THE PURPOSE OF OUR LIFE ON EARTH

Stanley Shinerock

Kingdom Publishers

Copyright© Stanley Shinerock 2025

All rights reserved. No part of this book may be reproduced in any form by photocopying or any electronic or mechanical means, including information storage or retrieval systems, without permission in writing from both the copyright owner and the publisher of the book. The right of Stanley Shinerock to be identified as the author of this work has been asserted by him in accordance with the Copyright, Designs, and Patents Act 1988 and any subsequent amendments thereto.

A catalogue record for this book is available from the British Library.

All Scripture quotations have been taken from the Douay-Rheims version of the Bible.

ISBN: 978-1-916801-00-4

1st Edition 2025 by
Kingdom Publishers, London, UK.

You can purchase copies of this book from any leading bookstore or at www.kingdompublishers.co.uk

DEDICATION

In memory of my dear wife, Mary E Shinerock, my companion in life for over 58 years

PUBLISHER'S NOTE

The reader may observe that the author has used lower case letters in many cases when referring to our Lord, and in other cases, capital letters. The reason for this is that the author has followed Scripture in which lower case letters are normally used. However, in his own writings, he has used capital letters. The same principle applies where he has quoted from other authors in his book.

Contents

ACKNOWLEDGEMENTS TO THE PUBLISHERS OF THE SPIRITUAL CLASSICS REFERRED TO IN MY BOOK OF ESSAYS	9
FIVE REFLECTIONS ON SUFFERING	11
ON ACCOUNTABILITY	15
THE THREE FACULTIES OF THE SOUL - AN ANALYSIS	20
ON THE DUAL NATURE OF MAN	22
THE DISPOSITIONS NECESSARY TO LEAD A LIFE OF PRAYER	36
SOME THOUGHTS ON FREE WILL	75
ON THE WILL OF GOD	81
FIGHT THE GOOD FIGHT WITH ALL THY MIGHT - CHRIST IS THY STRENGTH AND CHRIST THY LIGHT	89
THE IMPACT OF EVENTS IN THE MIDDLE EAST ON WORLD HISTORY	93
ON ADAM AND EVE	96
ON ADVENT AND LENT	105
ON THE RESURRECTION	112
SOME COMMENTS ON THE ARTICLE - DEPOSIT OF FAITH AND THE PRIESTHOOD	132
ON THE GREATNESS OF GOD AND THE LITTLENESS OF MAN	138
ON THE WORDS OF OUR LORD UTTERED IN THE GARDEN OF GETHSEMANI AND ON THE CROSS	151

I AM AT A LOSS WHAT TO DO	155
MY LAST WORD	163
ON THE UNDERSTANDING OF CERTAIN HARD SAYINGS IN MATTHEW 5:39/42	171
UNITY OF MAN	175
A SPIRITUAL CONUNDRUM	179
ON GENESIS - CHAPTERS 1 TO 5	183
A MYTH IS A FACT FORGOTTEN	185
A VERSE ON THE TRINITY	190
AUTHOR PROFILE	191

ACKNOWLEDGEMENTS TO THE PUBLISHERS OF THE SPIRITUAL CLASSICS REFERRED TO IN MY BOOK OF ESSAYS

Excerpts from **Loreto Publications:** The Douay-Rheims Bible

Excerpts from **Burns Oates & Washbourne:** (i) Ascent of Mount Carmel by St. John of the Cross, translated and edited and with an introduction by E. Allison Peers from the critical edition of P. Silverio de Santa Teresa, C.D. (ii) The Spirit of St. Francis de Sales by Jean Pierre Camus, Bishop of Belley.

Excerpts from **The Classics of Western Spirituality:** (i) Meister Eckhart: Teacher and Preacher, edited by Bernard McGinn, with the collaboration of Frank Tobin and Elvira Borgstadt, preface by Kenneth Northcott, Copyright © 1986 by Bernard McGinn, and from Francisco de Osuna: (ii) The Third Spiritual Alphabet, translated and with an introduction by Mary E. Giles; preface by Kieran Kavanaugh, OCD, Copyright 1981 by The Missionary Society of St. Paul the Apostle in the State of New York, published by Paulist Press, Inc. New York /Mahwah, NJ. Used with permission of Paulist Press [Paulistpress.com].

Excerpts from **Tan Books & Publishers Inc.:** (i) The Three Ages of the Interior Life and Our Savior and His Love for us by The Rev. R. Garrigou-Lagrange O.P., translated by Sister M. Timothea Doyle O.P. (ii) Treatise on the Love of God by St. Francis de Sales, translated and with an introduction by John K. Ryan.

Excerpts from Image Books - Doubleday: (i) Introduction to the Devout Life by St. Francis de Sales, translated and with an introduction and notes by John K. Ryan: (ii) The Dark Night of the Soul, The Living Flame of Love and The Spiritual Canticle, all by St. John of the Cross, translated by E. Allison Peers from the critical editions of P. Silverio de Santa Teresa, C.D. (iii) The Interior Castle and The Way of Perfection by St. Teresa of Avila and the Autobiography of St. Teresa, all translated by E. Allison Peers from the critical editions of P. Silverio de Santa Teresa, C.D.

Excerpts from Emmanuel Publications: Holy Communion by St. Peter Julian Eymard, translated by Clara Morris Rumball.

FIVE REFLECTIONS ON SUFFERING

Much has been written on suffering, its purpose and its meaning, yet it remains a mystery. A mystery that can only be solved by a soul when it plumbs the depths of God's love for humanity. The following five reflections observe certain characteristics of suffering in general.

First, it is part of the human condition, and is thus unavoidable. Go to any home, and ask if any of the persons living there has been free from suffering. We do not think you will receive a positive answer.

So we all suffer in one degree or another. This being the case, the question arises as to how we are to make the best use of it. Well, our Lord Jesus Christ showed us the way and gave the supreme example of what suffering is. He invites us to follow Him when He tells us to "take up our cross and follow Him." In fact, in Matthew 10:38/39, He is very specific when He says:

> "And He that taketh not up his cross and followeth Me, is not worthy of Me. He that findeth his life shall lose it, and he that shall lose his life for Me shall find it."

But we can see around us that suffering is universal, and we may ask if there is any difference between one who has no religious belief and one who has faith and trust in Jesus, since both are subject to this unavoidable condition of suffering.

There is an enormous difference between the two. The first suffers to no purpose and develops no higher life within him. The other has a marvellous opportunity to offer up his suffering in union with the suffering of our Lord. Note that in the quotation mentioned, Jesus specifies that "we must take up our cross and follow Him." From this, we may understand that to follow Him is to unite our suffering to His; then it becomes fruitful. For someone who suffers but has no belief or trust in God, the unavoidable suffering that life brings with it is barren, and so yields little or no fruit; in fact, if it does bear any fruit, it is likely to be bitter.

In some mysterious fashion, suffering is also tied to the (almost) superhuman virtue of forgiveness. People may say that only the saints have ever practised this virtue successfully, but that does not excuse us. If we never suffered, we would have nothing to forgive. In theory, we know this from the Lord's Prayer, which is also part of the celebration of the Mass, but unfortunately, the practice of this part of the Lord's Prayer lags far behind the theory. This is especially true in family relationships.

The second reflection on the mystery of suffering is that the pain experienced in suffering deepens the human personality in a profound way. This deepening enables us to endure the flux of day-to-day living, knowing that "this too, shall pass." It produces the fruits of patience and perseverance.

Let us take an example from Nature. Before the seeds of grain can be sown, which will eventually become the bread that we eat, the field must be ploughed. Now, if the soil could speak, it would probably complain bitterly of the pain experienced when the knives of the plough cut into it to turn over to produce the furrows into which is deposited the seeds. But without the pain of ploughing, there would be little chance for the seeds to take root, and thus sprout into wheat. Similarly, in some mysterious fashion, suffering creates furrows in the human soul into which seeds can be sown to produce the living virtues of faith and hope in addition to those of patience and perseverance.

The third reflection is that rightly understood, suffering purifies the soul; it gives it a distaste for the world and a longing for eternal happiness, which can only be found in God. A great Saint once said that when God created man, He left out happiness so that this lack would one day turn the face of man to the source of all happiness. Thus, suffering is also the water which nourishes the seeds which are planted in the furrows prepared for them.

The fourth reflection is that suffering is another name for sacrifice. Jesus tells us above that the one who seeks to save his life shall lose it, and the one who loses his life for Jesus' sake shall find it. To seek to save one's life is to sacrifice our time, resources, perhaps even a great advantage (in worldly terms) for the good of others. This is difficult, especially in the times in which we now live.

Nowhere is this attitude better exemplified than in the mother. (We are not here referring to the Blessed Virgin Mary, although she above all gave us the perfect example of true motherhood). A rabbi once told the story that when God created the world, He lacked one thing. He needed a person who would cook, wash, sew and do the one hundred and one things necessary for His children; even to be on hand twenty-four hours of the day for this purpose. The story goes that God could find no such person, and so He created the mother.

The fifth reflection is that the great Saints treat suffering as a gift, something in which to be joyful because they know that they suffer in union with the sufferings of Christ. This approach to suffering is God-given; it is an attitude that is beyond the comprehension of ordinary beings. With the Saints, the gift is a dual one because, as they accepted suffering as a gift from God, they in turn offer up their sufferings to God also as a gift, a gift which is most acceptable to Him. So what we can learn from this, is that suffering is an unsurpassed school of true love, in that it instructs us, not through human delights, but through the stripping away and renouncing of self on the Cross.

ON ACCOUNTABILITY

To be accountable to someone or for something is to take responsibility for what we do. This is fairly clear when we think about most situations in life in which personal accountability arises, and in such cases, we usually limit this to our words and actions, both as they affect others and society in general. This understanding may be satisfactory from the point of view of worldly affairs, but in our religious life (which impacts how we manage our affairs in this world) it is too narrow, too shallow, to be of much use in our spiritual life. For behind all words and actions are our thoughts, and it is these which govern our behaviour towards others. To control our thought patterns is to lay the foundation of control over our emotions, words and actions.

And herein lies the great difficulty of being accountable, because no one knows our thoughts except ourselves and God. Therefore, we are accountable to God first and then to others. We are especially accountable to those closest to us; children in having a respectful and obedient love for their parents, parents in caring for the physical, mental and spiritual needs of their children, husbands and wives in having a mutual and caring love for one another. The same applies to other relationships in different degrees, such as employees to their employer, the employer to its employees, governments to those whom they govern, and people to the society and country in which they dwell. Such accountability is what we understand from the commandment to love God with our whole heart, our whole soul, and our whole mind, and to love our neighbour as ourselves, which Jesus gave us in the Gospel according to St Matthew, thus restating the law which was first given in the Old Testament.

Being accountable in the manner just described is far easier said than done. For who is there who can control the spate of thoughts to which we are constantly subject? Virtually no one. There is only one way to do so, and this is to keep our minds and hearts in the presence of God within us as much as possible. Because this is an extremely difficult thing to do, the practice of prayer and mortification is the necessary training ground, and this is so whether we live in a monastery or in the world. For when one enters a monastery, one takes one's mind with one, and from our understanding, monasteries are not filled with saints. Therefore, there is little or no difference between the training ground of living our lives among family, friends, or colleagues in the workplace, all of which take place in the world, or living in a monastery. The only real difference is that the monastery environment is, or should be, subject to a strict Rule governing the religious life, and in those cases where the Rule has been eroded over time, as happened in the Carmelite Order for example, it takes a reform initiated by a strong-minding reformer such as St. Teresa of Avila to put things back on the right track.

It can be difficult for those who, living in the world, are subject to other persons living or working close to them (for example, members of the same family or colleagues in the workplace) and who do not wish to be accountable to God in the same way that they do. Here, the conflicts that arise are mostly due to different lifestyles, to different ways of thinking, and this can be so not only between different generations (parents and children) but also between husbands and wives, who as they get older, find themselves growing apart. It is in such situations that the word "accountable," which means to justify one's actions or decisions, takes on more subtle shades of meaning. Because, when we justify our behaviour, there is the tendency to distort the truth in order to prove that our position is the right one. This happened in the Franciscan Order, the spirituality of which started to decline even in the lifetime of St. Francis of Assisi. The result today is that there are three Franciscan Orders, and no doubt each one will justify their "accountability," which they will call their vocation, according to their own lights. However, it cannot be denied that St. Francis wrote only one Rule, and this fact was pointed out by St. Peter Julian

Eymard who, when speaking about the Rule governing a Religious Order in his work The Eucharist and Christian Perfection, said "God always blesses only the one whom He has chosen to lay the foundation, and never those who want to oppose him….No, God never blesses outside the first grace,…it is never permitted to change it, nor to introduce into it anything contrary to it."

Therefore, it is apparent from what we have said that it is easy to justify our "accountability" because of the weakness of our human nature. This even happened in the case of St. Peter, who was reproved by St. Paul for adopting what we should today call a double standard, when he ate with the Gentiles, but not in the presence of the Jews. (Galatians 2:11/14).

So what is the solution to this dilemma of the conflicts inherent in "accountability" from the point of view of the lay person, when even the Religious are not free from making errors in judgment? Well, we can turn to the great poet and playwright William Shakespeare for a good guide. In his play, Hamlet, we have some wonderful advice that is given by a father to his son, who was embarking on a new life. The father concludes his counsel by telling his son: "This above all; to thine own self be true: And it must follow, as the night the day, thou canst not then be false to any man…."

To be true to oneself is not possible unless we strive to obey the commandment of loving God and our neighbour. From what has been said, we know how difficult this can be, and from what the great apostle John said in his first Epistle, we know that we cannot love God, whom we cannot see unless we love our neighbour whom we can see. The question arises as to what is meant by loving our neighbour. As we understand it, such love has nothing to do with emotions or feelings. Indeed, I think that we might heartily dislike someone but the same time love him by wishing the best for him and praying for his spiritual well-being. This is to love someone with the love of charity. In its essence, charity is a spiritual love; it is a supernatural virtue and one that can only be practised by great self-denial. Very few of us there are who really love one another in a truly charitable manner.

Probably the most important virtue that comes to the aid of charity is simplicity. Simplicity knows no guile or deceit. The person who excels in this virtue is true to himself and thus is not false to any other man. Simplicity is the foundation stone of the great Religious Orders. In the religious life (whether in a monastery or the world), everything opposed to simplicity has to be rejected, especially as regards worldly needs. With the virtue of simplicity goes the virtue of discretion, and both of these admirable virtues are different aspects of the Cardinal virtue of Prudence.

We cannot truly be accountable to one another unless we practise, not only the Cardinal virtue of Prudence but also the other three Cardinal virtues of Justice, Fortitude and Temperance. And we cannot do this without the practice of mortification and prayer. How easy it is to think that we have mastered one or more of these virtues when in reality they slip through our fingers because of an overmastering passion, appetite or vice. When Christ tells us in the Book of the Apocalypse that we must be Overcomers (this word is mentioned eight times in the Apocalypse), He would not have said this if God were going to perform this work for us. Of course, we cannot become Overcomers without God's grace, but in order to draw His grace down upon us, we must show Him that we are intent on mastering our passions. This is what is meant by mortification, to put to death all that prevents us from being masters of ourselves. Mortification begins with the outer senses and progresses to the inner ones, which are dominated by our thought patterns and imagination. It is only when we begin to make progress in such virtues that it can become possible to fulfil the commandment of loving God with our whole heart, our whole soul, and our whole mind, and loving our neighbour as ourselves.

Since most of us tend to make one excuse or another in defense of our own ego, we may say: "Oh I appreciate what you say, but I simply don't have a gift for leading a religious life." This attitude is wrong, because we all possess the virtues within us, given by God as a gift, albeit in a latent form. This form has been described by theologians such as Fr. Garrigou-Lagrange as "Infused Virtues." But as with any gift, these virtues must be developed by personal effort and study, as is the case with many other things in life. Here, I refer the reader to Matthew: 25: 14/30 on the parable of the Talents. Verses 21/29 are particularly instructive, and it is appropriate to quote verse 29 in this regard:

"For to every one that hath shall be given, and he shall abound: but from him that hath not, that also which he seemeth to have shall be taken away."

To the extent that we fall short of the mark, we shall, as Jesus tells us in the Gospel according to St. Matthew, be cast into prison (i.e. Purgatory), and shall not go out from thence till we have repaid the last farthing, which represents the debt that we owe to God in regard to how we shall be held accountable to Him when this life of ours comes to an end.

THE THREE FACULTIES OF THE SOUL - AN ANALYSIS

*HIGHER ASPECT (INTERIOR MAN)	*LOWER ASPECT (EXTERIOR MAN)
MEMORY	
Self-awareness or knowledge of God within us, that dim consciousness that we are someone special or unique, which arises from the sense of I-Hood or Ego. When aligned with the higher aspects of the Understanding and the Will, we become fitting instruments of the Holy Spirit, vehicles of Grace, and truly able to help others	Functions in our activities related to the world. Keeps us bound to worldly desires by recalling the pleasure we have in them. When aligned with the lower aspects of the Understanding and the Will, generates conflict both inner and outer. These lower tendencies are fed by the passions and a corrupt imagination.
UNDERSTANDING	
Wisdom that is supernatural in its nature. An immediate knowledge of something acquired without mental labour. Reflects the Light of God's Intellect to a greater or lesser degree, depending on how much we conform to the Will of God	The reasoning faculty in man. Seeks the answers to life's problems and evolves solutions to them. When combined with the lower aspects of the Will and the Memory, the result is selfishness and greed, and one becomes prey to a corrupt imagination.
WILL	
The power within us that directs or channels the Memory and the Understanding. Through the exercise of the higher aspect of the Will, we become the master of our passions and make the imagination our servant	Seeks only its own benefit. Perverse in its expression. Corrupts the faculties of the Memory and the Understanding. We lose control of the imagination, with the result that we become further subject to the passions.

Comments

We strengthen the lower aspects of the Will, the Memory and the Understanding when we allow them to become caught up in the passions and the appetites of the body and the emotions. This in turn creates bad habits and low desires, which further weaken the Will. Once we become entangled in the downward spiral, we need a miracle to "convert" the Will to its higher aspects, and thus convert also the Memory and the Understanding. Hence the reason for prayer, discipline and mortification, which are invaluable and indispensable aids to direct our sense of uniqueness (referred to under the higher aspect of the Memory) within and thus commence the road towards sanctity. The Will, when caught up in the world, results in the expression of "egoism" or selfishness. This is one meaning of what Christ tells us: "The light of the body is the eye. If thy eye be single, thy whole body shall be lightsome; but if thy eye be evil, thy whole body shall be darksome. If then the light that is in thee be darkness: the darkness itself how great shall it be!" (Matthew 6:22/23.)

The only solution or road to "conversion" is prayer. When we pray, we exercise the higher aspects of the three faculties of the soul and thus move towards conversion. It is a slow process for most of us. Mental prayer, or meditation as it is also known, and contemplative prayer, are the most effective means in moving towards this conversion. Only these two types of prayer can control, and eventually purify, the imaginative faculty, which has been corrupted by the passions and the appetites.

*Based on the teachings contained in the "Ascent of Mount Carmel" by St. John of the Cross.

ON THE DUAL NATURE OF MAN

Introduction

The essay that follows is intended to say something about the dual nature of man, first, his lower part, which consists of his physical and mental make-up, and second his higher, or spiritual part. The spiritual part, though infinitely superior to the physical and mental parts, nevertheless needs the lower part so that the soul may, by overcoming the body's sensual nature, which includes the passions, rise above the lower part to take possession of its true inheritance as a child of God.

Speaking symbolically, the soul, having tasted of the Tree of Knowledge of good and evil mentioned in the second chapter of Genesis, may also take possession of the Tree of Life spoken of in the second and third chapters of Genesis and in the last chapter of the Apocalypse, by transcending its lower nature and rising up into its higher, supernatural nature. Our spiritual goal may further be illustrated by the teaching of the Church on what takes place in the rite of Baptism. At that time, the three theological virtues of Faith, Hope and Charity, the four moral virtues (also known as the Cardinal virtues) of Prudence, Justice, Fortitude and Temperance, and the gifts of the Holy Spirit were **infused** into the soul. By this, we mean that God has sown these virtues into the soul in much the same manner as a mighty oak tree is sown in a small seed. But just as the seed of an oak tree will not fructify unless it is implanted into the ground, and watered and nurtured with the proper ingredients that Nature provides, so neither will the virtues flower and grow in the soul unless they too are watered and nurtured. That is to say, these virtues must first be **acquired** through active effort on our part. Without such an active effort to acquire them, the infused virtues will remain in an undeveloped state, and the fact that they have been infused into the soul by God will not, in and by itself, make saints of us.

Because the infused virtues belong to the supernatural part of the soul, the ladder thereto must be climbed by the effort of the natural man in acquiring those virtues. And once this has been done, the power released into the soul by the infused virtues is much, much greater than the effect that the acquired virtues have on the life of the natural man. We cannot excuse ourselves by saying that we are not made of the stuff of saints. If we wish to develop our dual nature, we must follow the same pathway as that of the saints. In this regard, St. Francis de Sales tells us that although "Acts of the saints cannot be strictly imitated by people living in the world, yet they can be followed either closely or from a distance." Here, we should note that St. Francis gives preference to the word "closely."

It is only when the acquired virtues become part of our human nature that the infused virtues begin to flower in us. Therefore, we should always have our supernatural end in mind; otherwise, we may still remain a man rooted in the values of the world. Being good is often taken to be a virtue in itself, but it may simply be due to a placid temperament. We should also note that being good implies that we can also be much better. Being a good person is often equated with leading a good moral life, and if we do so, then, so the thinking goes, this is all that God requires of us. In what follows, we shall try to show that God demands much more from us.

To develop the spiritual part of our dual nature is also to show gratitude to our Lord. If we had a friend who had done us a great service, we would always be happy to be with him, even to go out of our way to do so. Well, who has done us a greater service than Jesus Christ! He is the Second Person of the Trinity, who assumed our miserable and sinful human nature in order to carry out His great Plan of Redemption, when He took on the filth of sin of Humanity, past, present and future, the cup He did not want to drink, in the garden of Gethsemani, finally offering Himself up on the

Cross as a holocaust immeasurably greater than all of the sacrifices described in the Old Testament. Thus, He redeemed our fallen human nature to make it possible for us to participate in His Divine Nature. Now, what greater Friend can we have than that! Would we not want to be in the company of such a Friend as much as possible in this life? How many of us can truly comprehend what He has done for us! I certainly cannot; I can appreciate it in an intellectual way, but I will be unable to plumb the depths of what He did for me unless I extend myself beyond being just a good person having good morals.

It is for these reasons that we must practise both prayer and mortification to develop the spiritual part of our dual nature. It is prayer that keeps our supernatural end always in view, and it is mortification that gives strength to the practice of the four moral virtues. Such then, is the true purpose of life; to sublimate the lower or human part of our dual nature in order to realise our higher and supernatural part. It is then that we truly begin to live the life of the three theological virtues of Faith, Hope and Charity.

Practical Considerations

We know from medical science that the physical nature of man is a most marvellous creation of God, and that man's mental faculties, his reasoning power and imagination, can be said to be more wonderful still, since by the use of these faculties, man has gained a great understanding, not only of his physical and mental make-up, but also of the physical universe in which we dwell. Such, then, is a description of the first part of the dual nature of man, and which is also the inferior part.

But it is on the second part of man's dual nature, his spiritual part, which far transcends his physical and mental make-up as the heavens are above the earth, that we wish to speak about. This spiritual part is spoken of in the first chapter of the Book of Genesis, which tells us that man was created in the image of God, and given dominion over the whole earth and everything in it. Our godlike nature is also mentioned in Psalm 81, wherein the psalmist says "You are gods, and all of you the sons of the most High." We also learn from the writings of the Saints that when we begin to develop the image of God within us, we can participate in God's very own Nature. To participate in God's own nature does not mean that we can become part of His Nature, for that is impossible since we are all creatures. But in the words of the great Spanish mystic, St. John of the Cross, it does mean that we can become God by participation. The great mystic Saints also explain that this second part of our dual nature contains three wonderful spiritual faculties, which are: the Understanding, the Will and the Memory.

The Understanding, of which man's reasoning power is only a pale reflection, participates in God's Intellect; the Will is intended to become one with God's Will, and the Memory is intended to dwell in God's timelessness, in which there is no past or future, but only the living present. In the sixth chapter of the Gospel according to St. John, our Lord tells us about the infinite superiority of the second part of our dual nature when He says:

> "It is the spirit that quickeneth: the flesh profiteth nothing. The words that I have spoken to you are spirit and life."

So the sole purpose of our life in the body is to develop this second and higher part of our dual nature. This does not mean that we must leave the world and become members of a religious order, but it does mean that in our position in life, be it in family or business affairs, we must live a moral and ethical life; in other words, a life of the highest integrity, and the higher the position of trust that we rise to in society, the greater is our responsibility to do so. This, then, is the first part of the foundation of developing the image of God within us.

The second part of this foundation is to develop a life of prayer. We do this when we set aside a part of each day for the sole purpose of placing ourselves in the Presence of God. Perhaps most of us think of prayer in terms of vocal prayer, saying the Rosary, for example. Vocal prayer, properly said, with full attention on what we are saying, and to whom we are speaking, raises our mind to God and helps to create an atmosphere of receptivity to His Presence. The most common difficulty with vocal prayers is that, although the tongue and lips recite them, the mind is far away, thinking of other things. It was for this reason that St. Teresa of Avila, another great Spanish mystic and a contemporary of St. John of the Cross, stated that in order to say one's vocal prayers properly, they must be accompanied by mental prayer, or meditation as it is also known. In her great work The Interior Castle, St. Teresa explains this dual nature of prayer when she tells us:

> "…..If a person does not think Whom he is addressing, and what he is asking for, and who it is that is asking and of Whom he is asking it, I do not consider that he is praying at all even though he be constantly moving his lips."

Thus, the great advantage of mental prayer combined with vocal prayer is that it fixes the attention on the subject matter of our prayer, be it the Rosary, a passage from Scripture, or even a loving conversation with God.

When one has been practising vocal prayer combined with mental prayer for some time, he may naturally find himself drawn to a silent repose, in which, as we have said, our heart and mind are lifted up to God. The Saints describe this as contemplative prayer or the prayer of recollection. In his Manual for Interior Souls, Fr. Jean-Nicholas Grou describes this prayer as "The Prayer of the Heart," which consists of a "Habitual and constant Disposition of Love to God." In his great work, the Ascent of Mount Carmel, St. John of the Cross describes contemplative prayer as

"….naught else than a secret, peaceful and loving infusion from God, which if it be permitted, enkindles the soul with the spirit of love….."

In describing the transition from vocal prayer to the prayer of recollection in his book Holy Communion, St. Peter Julian Eymard tells us how God acts within the soul:

"Then He changes the nature of its prayer. The soul is wearied by vocal prayer; it no longer finds therein the spiritual joy and fervor it once felt; it prays vocally from duty, not from desire. Books grow tiresome and offer no food that satisfies the heart; or, rather, the soul no longer understands them because they do not express its thought. Yet it feels withal a sweet and powerful attraction to inward prayer, to a prayer of silence, tranquillity, and peace in nearness to God. In this prayer of contemplation, the soul is divinely nourished…."

Further on in this book, St. Peter explains the value of interior prayer:

"When we pray, we do penance, practice self-mortification; we control our imagination, confine our will enchain our heart, humble our pride. Prayer is, therefore, holiness itself, since it includes the exercise of all the virtues.

Some say prayer is nothing but laziness! Very well. Take those who work hardest and always use their energies most eagerly; they will find it much more difficult to pray than they did to devote and sacrifice themselves to religious works. Ah, the fact is that it is sweeter, more consoling to nature, and easier to give to God than to ask of Him! ….

Just as the natural life depends on nourishment, so the supernatural life is absolutely dependent on prayer. Though you should be obliged to give up everything else, penance, religious labours, even Communion, never give up prayer! It belongs to every state in life and sanctifies them all. "What!" you ask. "Give up Communion, in which we receive Jesus Himself, rather than give up prayer?" Yes, for if you do not pray, this Sacrament in which Jesus comes to you will not diffuse its divine remedy within your soul. Without prayer, we are powerless to do any great thing for Jesus. Prayer invests us with His virtues; and if we do not pray, neither the saints nor God Himself will bring us forward on the road to sanctity. ......

The rudder which guides you and moves you is recollection. Do everything in your power to preserve it, or you will go adrift. Then, never say again: "Oh, what a holy soul! See how zealous this person is!" But, "Does he live the interior life?" If so, you may expect everything good from him; if not, he will come to nothing holy or great in the eyes of God. Therefore, be master of your exterior life; if it masters you, it will hurry you on to destruction. If your occupations leave you the opportunity to contemplate our Lord interiorly, you are on the right road; continue on it. If in the midst of action, your thoughts turn to God; if you know how to prevent interior dryness and desolation of heart; if your exterior labors always leave you tired and weary, yet conscious of a deep inner peace, oh, then, that is excellent! You are free and, beneath the eye of God, your own master."

Although our Lord gave us the Lord's Prayer, He gave few instructions on how to pray, but when He did so, it was contemplative prayer, or the prayer of recollection that He described in Matthew 6:6, when He said:

"But when thou shalt pray, enter into thy chamber, and having shut the door, pray to thy Father in secret: and thy Father who seeth in secret will repay thee."

And in Psalm 45:11, we are told:

"Be still and see that I am God. I will be exalted among the nations, and I will be exalted in the earth."

The two phrases: "exalted among the nations" and "exalted in the earth" mean that with God's help, we can still our unruly thoughts and exercise dominion over our passions and desires. This is what I believe our Lord spoke of when He said that we should "enter into the chamber (of the soul) and shut the door (of the bodily senses)."

So, the transition from vocal and mental prayer to contemplative prayer or the prayer of recollection is a very natural one. The soul will recognise the point of transition when it feels the desire just to remain peaceful and quiet, and to rest in God's Presence.

When we begin to exercise our spiritual faculties in developing the image of God within us, we commence to rise into our supernatural nature, and with God's help and grace, to claim our birthright as sons of God. No doubt this goal is the loftiest one that we could attempt in our earthly life, but as we have already said, we are on this earth for no other purpose notwithstanding the difficulties of leading a spiritual life amidst the pressing duties and responsibilities involved in our natural life.

But just as a coin has two sides, if we do not strive to develop the supernatural side of our soul by means of practising the virtues together with the science of prayer, then the baser side of our nature inherent in the natural man will exercise dominion over us. In his great work, the treatise On the Love of God, St Francis de Sales graphically describes the terrible state of a soul that allows the natural man to gain ascendance over his higher faculties:

> "Ancient philosophers recognised that there are two kinds of ecstasy, one of which raises us above ourselves while the other degrades us below ourselves. It is as if they meant that man is by nature midway

between angels and beasts; that in his intellectual part, he shares in the angelic nature, and in his sensitive part he shares in the nature of beasts; that by his life-conduct and by constant self-care he could still free and emancipate himself from his middle state; that by habituating and applying himself much to intellectual activities he might bring himself closer to the angels than to the beasts; that if he largely applied himself to sensual actions, he would descend from his middle state and approach that of the beasts; and that because an ecstasy is merely to go out of oneself, whichever path a man takes he is truly in ecstasy. Men who have been touched by **divine and intellectual pleasures** and have let their hearts be ravished by such feelings are truly outside of themselves, that is, they are above their natural condition. This is a blessed and desirable departure and by it they enter into a nobler and loftier estate. They are as much angels by the operation of their soul as they are men in natural substance, and they should be called human angels or angelic men. On the contrary, men who are allured by sensual pleasures and consign their souls to enjoyment of such things descend from their middle state to that of the lowest of brute beasts. To the same extent as they are by nature men, so do they deserve to be called brutish because of their actions. They are wretched when they go out of themselves in this way only to enter a condition infinitely unworthy of their natural state.

Now, according as an ecstasy is greater, whether that above us or that beneath us, so much the more does it hinder our soul from returning to itself and from performing acts contrary to the ecstasy in which it is. Hence as long as their ecstasy lasts those angelic men who are rapt up to God and heavenly things completely lose the use of sense, movement, and all exterior action. In order to apply its power and activity more entirely and attentively to that divine object, their soul draws this power or activity back and collects it from all its other faculties, so as to direct it in that way. In like manner, brutish men who have been ravished by sensual pleasure, and especially that of the sense of touch, completely lose use and control of reason and intellect. In order to sense most completely and acutely this brutish object, their unhappy soul turns away from spiritual activities so as to be turned to and buried in those which are bestial and brutish. …..

I say that when the soul makes love by sensual actions which thrust it down beneath itself, then of necessity the exercise of a higher love is so much the more weakened. Hence true, essential love is far from being aided and preserved by that union for which sensual love strives. On the contrary, it is weakened, dissipated, and ruined by such union. …..

Love that is of the heart and intellect, love that certainly is or should be master over our soul, rejects every kind of bodily and sensual union and is content with simple good will. The powers of the sensitive part, which are or should be handmaids of the spirit, demand, seek out, and seize what reason has rejected. Without obtaining leave, they run out and strive to achieve their abject, servile unions. In proportion as the soul turns to such gross, sensual unions, so far does it turn itself from a tender, intellectual, and heartfelt union. …..

So too love may be found in the unions of the sensual powers when they are intermingled with the unions of the intellectual powers, but never in so excellent a way as when the spirits and the souls alone, separated from all bodily affections but themselves united together, produce a pure, spiritual love. …..

There is no easier way to ruin love than to degrade it to base and earthly unions. 'Between spiritual and bodily pleasures, there is this difference,' says St. Gregory. 'Bodily pleasures arouse desire before we get them but disgust once we have obtained them. On the other hand, spiritual pleasures arouse disgust before we obtain them and pleasure once we have obtained them.' Thus animal love, which seeks to complete and perfect its complacence by the union it has obtained with its beloved object, finds contrariwise that in gaining this complacence it destroys it. Hence it becomes greatly disgusted with such a union. This has led the great philosopher (i.e. Aristotle) to say that after enjoyment of its most ardent and urgent physical pleasure, nearly every animal becomes sad, morose, and depressed. It is like a tradesman who had hoped to reap a great profit but finds himself plunged down and caught in a severe loss. On the contrary, in the union it achieves with its object intellectual love discovers more satisfaction than it had hoped for. It perfects its complacence therein and continues it by uniting with it, and by such continuance is united ever more closely with it." {Note: The word "complacence" appears to be an error in translation. It should be read as "complaisance"}

In the development of his treatise On the Love of God, St. Francis de Sales makes it abundantly clear that true intellectual activity is founded upon a life of prayer and mortification. If these are not practised, then this will result in spurious fruits of the intellect and the imagination, which will end up by feeding man's sensual nature.

When he speaks about intellectual activities bringing man closer to the angels than to the beasts, St. Francis is not referring to the intellect as it manifests itself in the lesser expression of man's reasoning power, but rather to the raising of his reason to the higher reaches of the spiritual faculty of the Understanding. This is made clear by the wording 'divine and intellectual pleasures' highlighted on page 30. Nor do such intellectual activities refer to mere theological study, although such study may be a fruit of such activities provided they are founded upon prayer and mortification. This is not to say that we must exclude culture, as exemplified in the arts and sciences from man's intellectual activities, but rather to point out that in the thought of St. Francis de Sales and other great spiritual men and women, if the animal man is not made subservient to the higher and supernatural part of man's soul, then the expression of man's creative imagination in the arts and sciences will become debased and bestial.

Let us again reflect on the words in the first chapter of the Book of Genesis, that man was created in the image of God, and given dominion over the whole earth and everything in it. Man was given dominion over the whole earth and everything in it provided that he continued to be true to his being created in the image of God. If he ignores the higher part of his dual nature, and lives only for his animal nature, the image of God is obscured within him; then spiritual anarchy will be the result, and all his fine plans and projects will end up in chaos.

One would have to be wilfully blind not to recognize in our modern-day society the clear signs of man's descent into his animal nature, and its terrible fruits. The culture of pleasure and freedom of expression at any cost is the dominant factor in society; drugs, both organic and synthetic, destroy the body and mind of those who are drawn into their seductive appeal; sex is everywhere paraded as a god to be worshipped; the absolute values set forth in the Ten Commandments are scorned, and greed, corruption and violent crime are the inevitable results of such freedom of expression.

All of this has come about solely because man has rejected God from his equation of living, and more particularly, the Christian world has largely rejected Christ. Yes, the outer form of Christian worship may still exist in its various denominations, but that is the husk; the kernel of spiritual discipline in the form of sacrificial prayer and the spiritual discipline of the mortification of the sensual nature as described by St. Francis de Sales and St. Peter Julian Eymard and other great Saints, has all but disappeared. The direct result of this is that the image of God has become buried deep within man's sensual nature, and man's reason, which as we have said above is but a pale reflection of the God-given spiritual faculty of the Understanding, has become irretrievably darkened.

As proof that we are indeed created in the image of God, many of us can recall having had that indefinable feeling of a longing for something that we know not what. We do not know from whence this feeling comes, but somehow, it resonates deep within us. Since we are made in the image of God, our source lies in Him, so it is possible that this feeling arises from that source. However, an image of something is not that something itself, but partakes of it. In the same way, we partake of God's own Nature, but we are not of that Nature. This is what St. Paul meant when he said that we have received the spirit of adoption of sons. It is this partaking of, or image of God's Nature, that creates within us a longing to return to Him, no matter how faint. Sometimes this longing arises when we take a walk in beautiful countryside, or when we gaze out over the seemingly infinite expanse of the ocean, or when we listen to a great symphony. It can arise when we pray, whether in a church or in our own home. If we experience this longing in prayer, then it is safe to say that it is the call of the Holy Spirit, awakening in our souls that intimacy with God that, as St. Paul says, makes us, if sons, then heirs also. To experience such blissful moments, we must remove from our souls as much of earthly attachments as we can by our own efforts, aided by grace. This grace will always be forthcoming provided that we do not give up the struggle, for in the words of St. John of the Cross in the Ascent of Mount Carmel:

> "Upon this road, we must ever journey in order to attain our goal, which means that we must ever be mortifying our desires and not indulging in them; and if they are not all completely mortified we shall not completely attain….."

So, I conclude that being a good, moral person is not good enough, for as already mentioned on page 23, this may be due to having a placid temperament, and this is a far cry from the holiness that Jesus calls us to in the Sermon on the Mount. We must put the precepts He taught us into practice to the best that lies in us, realising that we can always do better. This requires effort and perseverance, and in this regard, we should bear in mind that God will not be outdone in generosity. He will give us the gift of fortitude and whatever other gifts He sees are good for us if we just have a willing will. We do not get nourishment from a good meal for our physical bodies simply by admiring it; we must eat it. The Saints ate their spiritual meals of penance, mortification and prayer with a gusto that we may not be able to imitate. However, as St. Francis de Sales tells us in his Introduction to the Devout Life, we can follow them closely or from a distance.

THE DISPOSITIONS NECESSARY TO LEAD A LIFE OF PRAYER

Introduction

I have nothing to tell you of myself, but I am content to share the knowledge that I have gained by reading the works of the great spiritual masters over many years, as well as Scripture. In considering the great importance of the subject of prayer, one thing that has become clear to me is the necessity of developing the right dispositions so that we can profit from this spiritual exercise, the ultimate goal of which is union with God Himself. While very few enter the higher mansions described by St Teresa of Avila in her book the 'Interior Castle,' many of us can, by developing the right dispositions (which is nothing less than practising the virtues, of which much more will be said below), make significant progress before the great change, which we call death, takes place. If we keep this inexorable fact ever before us, then this will be an added spur to work on ourselves before this change takes place. In order to emphasise the material to which I refer, I will occasionally repeat quotations from Scripture and from the works of the Saints and other great writers on spirituality as the context of this essay so requires. I ask the reader to forgive me if I seem overly prolix, but the subject on which I am writing is so important that I consider repeating such quotations is of more value than to omit them.

Success in any endeavour in life requires that we develop the right attitudes and skills. This is more true on the subject of prayer than on any other subject. The reason for this is that it concerns our soul, which is intended by God to possess and enjoy Him for eternity, and the writings of the Saints tell us that we were created and placed on this earth for no other purpose. If a mountaineer could transmute his tenacity in climbing mountains to conquering himself, he would become a Saint in short order.

The same thing can be said of all who achieve success and fame in any worldly pursuit, be it in politics, sport, or business, all of which are fleeting, and are of no lasting worth. The opposite is the case with spirituality, as I shall try to show in what follows.

When we place ourselves in an attitude of prayer, we are giving time to God; we are placing ourselves at His disposal. But some people will say (and this is very prevalent in the times in which we live) that: "We have no time for prayer——there will be plenty of time for that when we retire from work, and when our children are raised. God wants us to enjoy life; He hasn't created us to be monks." Such people should take note of what is said in Ecclesiasticus 25:5:

> "The things that thou hast not gathered in thy youth, how shalt thou find them in thy old age?"

We should listen even more to what Jesus tells us in John 6:64, Matthew 6:24 and 16:24/26, and Luke 12:31:

> "It is the spirit that quickeneth: the flesh profiteth nothing. The words that I have spoken to you are spirit and life. [John 6:64]"

> "No man can serve two masters. For either he will hate the one, and love the other: or he will sustain the one, and despise the other. You cannot serve God and mammon. [Matthew 6:24]"

> "Then Jesus said to his disciples: If any man will come after me, let him deny himself, and take up his cross, and follow me. For he that will save his life, shall lose it: and he that shall lose his life for my sake, shall find it. For what does it profit a man, if he gains the whole world, and suffer the loss of his own soul? Or what exchange shall a man give for his soul? [Matthew 16:24/26]"

"But seek ye first the kingdom of God and his justice, and all these things shall be added unto you. [Luke 12:31]"

I would like to offer the following illustration on how I understand the meaning of our Lord's words quoted above.

There are basically two classes of souls; those who pray and those who do not. Let us take the image of a burning candle to describe both classes. The soul that prays is like a candle that burns in an upright position. The flame of a candle that is burning as it should is absolutely clear and bright; it hardly seems to be attached to the body of the candle at all. The flame uses the wax of the body as its fuel, and the more the body of the candle is consumed, the clearer and brighter the flame burns. The entire duty of the body of the candle is to sacrifice itself for the flame. However, not all candles burn as perfectly as the one just described. It is often necessary to cut the body of the candle here, and to trim the wick there if the candle gives off too much smoke, in order to ensure that the flame will not go out, but will burn increasingly clearer and brighter. In like manner, we are to discipline our body, mind and emotions so that over time, the candle flame of our soul will not go out, but will burn ever more strongly in love of God. This means that together with prayer, we must develop and practise the virtues, for if both do not go hand in hand, then as St Teresa of Avila tells us in her work the 'Interior Castle', we will never grow more than dwarfs.

We can also use the image of a burning candle to describe a soul that does not pray. A soul that does not pray is like a candle that burns upside down. The flame may, like a candle burning in an upright position, burn strongly, but it will not burn clear of the body of the candle but will attack the body. The flame will smoke, it will sputter, and after destroying the body of the candle, it will go out.

There are also souls who fall somewhere between the two classes of souls described above. They pray, but only intermittently; they also consider that it is only necessary to fulfil the minimum obligations of religious worship in an exterior fashion through attendance at Church once a week. If such souls put just one tenth of the time that they invest in other interests to widening their spiritual horizons as will be explained below, they would gain far more profit for themselves.

We should also bear in mind the words of St. Augustine in regard to our duty to God in setting aside time for prayer. He tells us that: "God who created you without yourself, will not sanctify you without yourself." Also, in the closing words of his work 'The Third Spiritual Alphabet', we are told by Francisco Osuna that: "Consider that God created you for no other purpose than prayer, nor does he ask of you anything except that you pray to him in spirit and in truth, for in this way there will quicken in you concern to complete your task and become master of it….."

On the Meaning of the word 'Disposition'

The Concise Oxford Dictionary tells us that the word 'Disposition' means:

"(i) A person's inherent qualities of mind and character. (ii) An inclination or tendency."

The first meaning describes what we are at any given time during our lives, and the second one describes those attributes that contribute towards moulding our mind and character. Here, one may note that the word 'inclination' means a natural tendency or urge to act or feel in a particular way. Clearly then, our dispositions change over time in accordance with the effort and discipline we put in to achieve our goals in life. We have only to read the lives of the Saints to see how they worked on themselves with the result that they changed their dispositions from that of ordinary men and women to that of high degrees of sanctity. The more effort they made, the more grace they received from God, and what they did, God also expects us to attempt. We may not become saints, but as Saint Francis de Sales tells us:

> "Acts of the saints cannot be strictly imitated by people living in the world, yet they can be followed either closely or from a distance."

This principle should be kept in mind in what follows, for if we are to develop the right dispositions to lead a life of prayer, then we cannot do less than make the necessary effort if we desire to enter the 'narrow gate' spoken of by Jesus in Matthew 7:13/14, wherein He says:

> "Enter ye in at the narrow gate: for wide is the gate, and broad is the way that leadeth to destruction, and many there are who go in thereat. How narrow is the gate, and strait is the way that leadeth to life: and few there are that find it!"

But before we throw up our hands in despair after reading the above verses, telling ourselves that the game of acquiring the necessary dispositions for spiritual progress is not worth the candle of the likelihood of succeeding to any degree, we should remember the words of the disciples: "Who then can be saved?", in response to our Lord's words: "It is easier for a camel to pass through the eye of a needle, than for a rich man to enter into the kingdom of heaven." We can take comfort from our Lord's answer: "With men this is impossible: but with God all things are possible." [Matthew 19:24/26]. Since effort and grace go hand in hand, we all have a duty to try to enter into the 'narrow gate', and although we may fail to do so in the manner of the Saints, we should have the satisfaction of doing our best. What we do not do here in the body, God will accomplish for us in the purification of our soul that takes place in Purgatory after death. In truth, and according to the teachings of St. John of the Cross in his work 'The Dark Night of the Soul', there are very few souls who enter through the 'narrow gate', which is to undergo the passive purification or the night of the spirit described by the saint in that work.

At this point, some might raise the objection that developing the right disposition for a life of prayer is surely the vocation of those who have chosen to enter religious orders. I would reply that, yes, such a way of life is incumbent on those who choose such a vocation. But I would also insist that God calls all to such vocation in accordance with their status and position in life. Do not all possess a soul? In Genesis 1:27, we are told that we are all made in the image of God. Also, Jesus Himself tells us in Matthew 5:48 that: "Be you therefore perfect, as also your heavenly Father is perfect". Jesus gave this commandment to all, not just to His immediate disciples. This commandment was also given to Israel, as set out in the Old Testament, for in Leviticus 19:2, the Lord spoke to Moses, saying: "Speak to all the congregation of the children of Israel, and thou shalt say to them: "Be ye holy, because I the Lord your God am holy." And God affirmed this commandment in Deuteronomy 18:13, saying: "Thou shalt be perfect, and without spot before the Lord thy God."

Therefore, if we can agree on these basic principles, then it must be admitted that all have a duty to become religious to some degree. And the time and place to do this is in this life, for it is a principle of Catholic theology that one can only gain merit while we live since after death one can no longer earn merit or incur demerit. [This doctrine is explained in the book 'Life Everlasting', by the great Dominican theologian, Fr. Garrigou-Lagrange.] Also, the great theologians of the Church tell us that if we wish to get the maximum benefit from Holy Communion and the Sacrament of Penance, it is very necessary to develop the right dispositions, which embrace the virtues.

Included under the umbrella of 'right dispositions' is the practice of mortification. Another name for 'mortification' is 'austerity'. This is what Jesus taught us in Matthew 16:24/25, wherein He said:

"If any man will come after me, let him deny himself, and take up his cross, and follow me. For he that will save his life, shall lose it; and he that shall lose his life for my sake, shall find it."

In a work entitled 'The Secret of Sanctity', Fr. Crasset, a well-known spiritual writer in the 17th century, tells us in writing on the uses of mortification, that:

".... there can be no interior mortification without exterior [mortification]; and this last must come first. In a word, to be spiritual, bodily mortification is indispensable. ....

Our life may be estimated by our prayer, and our prayer by our mortification. ..... Without exterior mortification, it is idle to expect that we shall ever attain the higher grace of interior mortification. It is the greatest of delusions to suppose that we can mortify judgment and will if we do not mortify our body also. ....The tenth and last use of mortification is that it is a most excellent school for the queenly virtue of discretion. The truly mortified man will as little think of not listening to discretion as he would think of listening to cowardice."

In relation to prayer, Fr Crasset also states that:

"We find innumerable precepts concerning prayer in books; the shortest way, in my opinion, is that of detachment and mortification. ....Therefore, to rise to heaven we must be detached from earth, and to unite ourselves with God in prayer we must separate ourselves, by mortification, from all creatures. ..... How can we practise mortification if we do not know how to pray, you ask? For prayer is as necessary to mortification as mortification is to prayer. True, and for that reason they must never be separated; however painful and laborious we find prayer, we must never abandon it, inasmuch as this labor is very great mortification."

In referring to prayer and mortification, St. Francis de Sales reminds us that:

> "Interior and exterior mortification is a powerful means to draw down upon us the favours of Heaven if we practise it in charity and through charity. Mortification without prayer is a body without a soul, and prayer without mortification is a soul without a body." [Introduction to the Devout Life].

The understanding that we can draw from the above is that the motive of our exterior and interior mortifications must be the love of God, or as St. Francis de Sales puts it, 'in charity and through charity', and that this is a powerful means to draw down upon us the favours of heaven. He also says that the greatest mortifications are not the best, declaring that ordinary ones, which fall to our lot daily and unexpectedly, are more fruitful and assure the conformity of our will to God's will. Nevertheless, until we have become the master of the outer appetites, it is a delusion to think that we can overcome the capital sins of pride, anger, lust, gluttony, avarice, envy, and sloth. These capital sins come under the 'concupiscence of the flesh', the 'concupiscence' of the eyes', and the 'pride of life', described by St. John the Apostle in his First Epistle. In his 'Dark Night of the Soul', St. John of the Cross tells us that ".... all the imperfections and disorders of the sensual part (of the soul) have their strength and root in the spirit, where all habits, both good and bad, are brought into subjection, and thus, until these are purged, the rebellions and the depravities of sense cannot be purged thoroughly". Many of these disorders are purged away under the night of sense, as described by St John of the Cross, but others, especially those that come under the 'pride of life', must be purged away in the night of the spirit, also described by St. John of the Cross. The pity of it is that we rarely give a thought to such things, but continue to spend our time in exterior activities as though we had a thousand years to develop an inner life of prayer. Indeed, modern-day society is based on those very things which are so destructive to our spiritual good. The result is that our lives lack simplicity, and we carry on in this way until we find ourselves in a hospital bed waiting for death to release the soul from the body to go to it knows not where without having made hardly any effort to develop our interior life.

In regard to exterior mortification, specifically on the discipline of the palate, Francisco Osuna tells us in his work the Third Spiritual Alphabet:

"….. Eat only what is necessary for your health and physical needs; above all, kill the desire for food, because gluttony is more desire than action, as seen in Esau, who sinned in greed when he coveted coarse food excessively. ….If you practise recollection, eventually you will lose the desire for food and take no pleasure in eating. This will not be some kind of malady, but the consequence of having tasted the Spirit, the flavor of which makes all meat taste insipid by comparison. …. You should prefer the cheapest and most ordinary food unless your physical needs and condition dictate otherwise, and eat only those that are easily digested."

An important topic to be discussed on the meaning of the word "Disposition" is the great value of spiritual reading. We widen our spiritual horizon through spiritual reading; books written by those who have experienced what they write about convey not only the understanding of the writer but also his life impulse. In his classic work 'The Three Ages of the Interior Life - Volume One', Fr. Garrigou-Lagrange tells us in a chapter devoted to spiritual reading that:

"Among the great means of sanctification offered to all, should be included spiritual reading, especially that of Holy Scripture, of the works of the masters of the interior life, and the lives of the saints. …. Next to the Scriptures, the reading of the spiritual works of the saints greatly enlightens and warms the soul, because these works, though not composed under infallible inspiration, were written with the lights and unction of the Holy Ghost. …. We must also, with a sincere and keen desire for perfection, apply to ourselves what we have read, instead of being content with a theoretical knowledge of it. …. If beginners and the advanced have a keen desire to sanctify themselves, they will find what is suitable for them in Holy Scripture and in the spiritual writings of the saints. While reading, they will hear the teaching of the interior Master. That this may be so, they must read slowly and not devour books; they must be penetrated with what they read. …."

Fr. Garrigou-Lagrange adds towards the end of the chapter referred to above:

"It is also well after a few years to reread the very good books which have already done us much good. Life is short: we should be content to read and read again whatever bears the mark of God, and not to lose our time on things that are lifeless and have no value. St. Thomas Aquinas never wearied of rereading the conferences of Cassian. How many souls have gained greatly by often rereading The Imitation? To be profoundly penetrated by one such book is far better than to reread all spiritual writers superficially."

In The Secret of Sanctity, Fr. Crasset says:

"Seek the books and preachers who touch your hearts and not those who flatter your ear. Never let a day pass without reading a good book. Reading, says St. Bernard, seeks God; meditation finds Him; contemplation enjoys Him. Reading helps meditation, and meditation leads to contemplation. If you like the end, adopt the means; if you desire to taste heavenly things, frequently read and meditate upon them."

So, it is clear that spiritual reading continued throughout one's lifetime is essential to both understanding and developing the dispositions necessary to practise a life of prayer. Such reading gives an intimacy with the subject of spirituality that nothing else, other than a direct experience of the operation of God in our life, can give. Attending talks or lectures on the subject can help; they can provide an impetus to our desire to know God, but they will soon fade from our memory unless we translate what we hear into positive action.

We will now consider the virtues to be practised in order to develop the right dispositions for a life of prayer.

On the Virtues, and how their Practice is essential to developing the right Dispositions.

Although St. Teresa of Avila wrote her famous work, the Interior Castle, for the nuns of her Order, it applies to all who wish to make spiritual progress. In pointing out that we cannot please God by words alone, St. Teresa wrote in relation to prayer that:

> ". ..... You must not build upon foundations of prayer and contemplation alone, for, unless you strive after the virtues and practise them, you will never grow more than dwarfs. God grant that nothing worse than this may happen - for, as you know, anyone who fails to go forward begins to go back, and love, I believe, can never be content to stay for long where it is."

In the Three Ages of Interior Life – Volume One, Fr. Garrigou-Lagrange describes the spiritual organism as consisting of the three theological virtues of faith, hope, and charity; the four cardinal virtues of prudence, justice, fortitude, and temperance; and the seven gifts of the Holy Spirit of wisdom, understanding, knowledge, counsel, piety, fortitude, and fear. For the purpose of this essay, we will concentrate on the four cardinal virtues.

In Volume Two of the Three Ages of the Interior Life, Fr. Garrigou-Lagrange explains that the word 'cardinal' is derived from its Latin equivalent, meaning 'hinges'. Thus, the four cardinal virtues of prudence, justice, temperance and fortitude are likened to the four hinges of a double-door [which Fr. Garrigou-Lagrange calls the 'temple door'], which we can also liken to the soul, because just as a double-door needs all four hinges to hang properly, and to be fully secure, so the soul needs all four virtues to develop a vibrant, spiritual life. Success in practising the cardinal virtues is very much dependent on the virtue of humility since this virtue is the foundation of the spiritual life. It is here that the saints excelled, and most of us lack. In Matthew 10:16, our Lord says that: "Be ye therefore wise as serpents and simple as doves." To be wise is to develop the virtue of prudence; to be simple is to lack guile and all human cunning, for in this manner we will be more receptive to the Holy Spirit.

Fr. Garrigou-Lagrange tells us that the two upper hinges on the temple door symbolize prudence and justice, which are in the higher part of the soul, and the two lower hinges are figures of fortitude and temperance, which have their seat in the sensible appetites, common alike to man and animal. To prudence are attached foresight, steadfastness, and constancy. To justice are attached religion, which renders to God the worship due to Him; penance, which offers Him reparation for offenses committed against Him, and obedience, which makes man obey the divine commandments and the direction of the spiritual or temporal representatives of God. To fortitude are attached patience, which enables us to endure daily vexations without weakening; magnanimity, which permits us to accomplish great things without becoming discouraged; and longanimity, which makes us bear incessant difficulties or contradictions that sometimes can continue for many years. To temperance are attached chastity; meekness, which moderates irritation or anger, and poverty, which makes us use the things of the world without becoming attached to them.

Prudence directs the other three virtues of justice, temperance, and fortitude, moderates their excesses, and corrects their laxities. We develop discrimination and discretion from the virtue of prudence, and when we faithfully keep up the discipline of prayer, which is aided by the virtue of fortitude, we can, with the grace of God, be given discernment, which is a very high order of prudence, and which is the beginning of wisdom. Discernment helps us to consider everything from the transcendent viewpoint of the soul's relationship with God. False prudence, on the other hand, is described by Fr. Garrigou-Lagrange as 'the wisdom of the flesh', and degenerates into slyness or cunning. This false prudence is foolishness and a delusion, for as St. Paul tells us in 1 Corinthians 3:19: "The wisdom of this world is foolishness with God." Thus, false prudence is the shrewdness of the worldly man, and in Ecclesiasticus 21:24, we find:

"Learning to the prudent is an ornament of gold, and like a bracelet upon his right arm."

The virtue of prudence, when faithfully practised, results in the gift of counsel. Similarly, when we practise the virtue of fortitude, especially in our prayer life, we will be given the gift of fortitude, for without both the virtue and gift of fortitude, a life of sustained prayer is not possible. This last is a wonderful thing, for even when we suffer in great aridity in our prayer life, the gift of fortitude keeps us faithful to its practice. We can earn great merit from this dual aspect of fortitude.

One thing we can learn from the practice of the cardinal virtues and this is that we can do little or nothing without God's help. When this is truly instilled in us, we then begin to develop the virtue of humility, which as mentioned above, is the foundation of the spiritual life, for without it, we cannot develop a true relationship with God. That God loves the humble and detests the proud is testified to in Isaias: 40:4, wherein it is said:

"Every valley shall be exalted, and every mountain and hill shall be made low, and the crooked shall become straight, and the rough ways plain."

St. Paul is a perfect example of the soul who went out to seek God; after his conversion, his entire life was a mortification of mind, body and soul. He was an example of the very words he wrote in Romans 8:13:

"For if you live according to the flesh, you shall die: but if by the Spirit you mortify the deeds of the flesh, you shall live."

In the lives of the saints in the Catholic tradition, we will find that they were living examples of these teachings. As for ordinary people like us, although we may not be able to rise to the peak of sacrifice offered by such souls, it is still our duty to conform ourselves to the teachings of our Lord so far as in us lies. We cannot expect to rise to the 'third heaven' if we lead merely earthly lives, and we have no guarantee that we shall inherit such a high spiritual state after death. I am not referring to extraordinary penances, but to those daily opportunities we have to practise mortification and self-restraint in every aspect of our lives, in the situations we encounter and the people we meet, in our emotions and our appetites. There is no lack of such situations in which we can practise these disciplines. In this regard, a perfect guide for the lay person who is serious about wishing to make spiritual progress is the Introduction to the Devout Life, written by St. Francis de Sales for a penitent of his who, due to her position in society, was obliged to lead much of her life among the royalty of the French court. In this book, St. Francis covers every aspect of life lived in the world, and in the second part of the Introduction, he tells us that while:

"Acts of the saints cannot be strictly imitated by people living in the world, yet they can be followed either closely or from a distance."

To know God is to become like Him, to conform ourselves to His nature, and the two virtues that are key to this are humility and purity. For most of us, this is a work of a lifetime, and yet if we strive to develop such virtues God will not fail, when we come before Him in prayer, to infuse those very qualities in us that He Himself possesses. If we do not give up the struggle in the short term, then God will grant us the gift of perseverance in the long term. In Chapter 4 of the Canticle of Canticles, the Bridegroom says to the spouse:

> "Thou hast wounded my heart, my sister, my spouse, thou hast wounded my heart with one of thy eyes, and with one hair of thy neck."

This wound can be said to consist of the sincere desire of the soul to know its Creator and the effort to overcome its faults, in which the soul makes its very failures to be stepping stones on the rocky path of life. Likewise, it can also be said that because of this wound given by the soul to God, in return God likewise wounds the soul with the gift of perseverance, in which the soul then exclaims with Job:

> "Although he should kill me, I will trust in him: but yet I will reprove my ways in his sight."

It is because of this wound given by God to the soul that it can never give up the struggle, even up to its last breath of life in this world.

In the Sermon on the Mount, as recorded in Matthew Chapters 5/7, Jesus gave His first teaching, not only to His disciples but also to the multitudes that followed Him. This is made clear in Matthew 7:28/29, wherein it is said:

"And it came to pass when Jesus had fully ended these words, the people were in admiration at his doctrine. For he was teaching them as one having power, and not as the scribes and Pharisees."

Jesus gave the highest teachings in this Sermon, which are intended to make saints of us all, not just members of the clergy and religious; as God, He could do no less. Let us consider the following verses from the Sermon in the Gospel according to St. Matthew:

"Blessed are the clean of heart; for they shall see God." [5:8]

"And if thy right eye scandalize thee, pluck it out and cast it from thee. For it is expedient for thee that one of thy members should perish, rather than that thy whole body be cast into hell. And if thy right hand scandalize thee, cut it off, and cast it from thee: for it is expedient for thee that one of thy members should perish, rather than that thy whole body go into hell." [5:29/30]

"Be you therefore perfect, as also your heavenly Father is perfect." [5:48]

Now, these seem to be extraordinary teachings to place before the people, but I do not think that Jesus would have given them had He not known that there were some present who would take advantage of them, those who would not, in the words of Matthew 7:28, just be 'in admiration at his doctrine'. This can also be said of many souls in the succeeding centuries who would take a good look at themselves, and realise that their righteousness, as the prophet Isaias said, was like a filthy rag.

If we consider the worth of our soul, that it was created in the image of God, as we are told in Genesis 1:27, the teachings of Jesus no longer become extraordinary. As we have said above, two virtues which today's society has little use for are humility and purity, but both of these are essential if we wish to achieve progress on the way which will make us friends of God. These virtues are most effectively developed in our youth, for it is false philosophy to tell ourselves that God can wait because our first priority is to enjoy life to the full. Ecclesiasticus 25:5 tells us that:

> "The things that thou hast not gathered in thy youth, how shalt thou find them in thy old age?"

The value of curtailing our passions and desires when we are young is that we are then making God an acceptable offering. It is not acceptable to Him if we live a worldly life, and then in our middle age, when we have exhausted most of our passions and energies, to say that: 'Now, God, we will give some time to You'. Any reasonable person who is offered a gift of something second or third-hand would not be pleased with it; similarly, it is no gift to God to offer Him a worn-out shell. And if we consider the matter, if we offer God our best in our youth, are we not offering Him something which we first received from Him as a free gift! Indeed, we must figuratively speaking, sometimes 'pluck out our right eye or cut off our right hand' if we want to avoid those things that would be to our spiritual detriment. This is especially true in the times in which we live, for a glance at the ways of the world today shows that humanity has made little or no progress towards this desirable goal. This is because we have sullied, covered over the soul's noble faculties of the understanding and the will with the grime of excessive indulgence of our sensual nature in worldly pleasures, with the result that the memory and the imagination are filled with negative influences that draw us into worldly desires, which further cause the deterioration of these faculties. But it is never too late, even though we are well past our youth, for whatever we do to please Him while in the body God will reward us one hundredfold, for somewhere it has been said that God will not be outdone in generosity.

Many may agree with the necessity of trying to lead a spiritual life that is superior to just being a good moral person, but will say that this will take up much of their lives. There are so many calls on our time and energy just in the ordinary business of living that, even if we wished to spend more time in the pursuit of our spiritual development, the burdens of our jobs, our families, and the need to clothe, feed and give rest to our bodies leave us with little time to spare. Thus, it becomes strictly a matter of choice, or the exercise of our free will, as to how we use this spare time. This taskmaster of 'necessity' infuses in us a corresponding need for relaxation and enjoyment. If we suggest to others that relaxation and enjoyment can also be found in reading the lives of the saints and other uplifting spiritual writings, in studying Scripture, and in quiet prayer, just as much, if not more, than can be found in reading a good novel, watching a good movie, or listening to uplifting music, it is doubtful if we would be taken seriously. Here, one can make the point that to do the first need not rule out the second. However, there is no doubt that the first is to our greater profit. Reading good literature, and listening to the most profound and beautiful music may or may not make us better persons; this is far more likely to happen if we give some time to our religious development. It may be possible to have our cake and eat it too, but we must be very disciplined if we do so. Again, it is appropriate to consider the teachings given by Jesus quoted above on 'plucking out our right eye and cutting off our right hand', and on 'taking up our cross and following Him'. The following verses from Ecclesiasticus, the Epistle of St. Paul to the Romans, his first Epistle to the Corinthians, his Epistle to the Galatians, and his Epistle to the Ephesians are also relevant:

"God made man from the beginning and left him in the hand of his own counsel. Before man is life and death, good and evil, that which he shall choose shall be given him." [Ecclesiaticus 15:14-18]

"For if you live according to the flesh, you shall die: but if by the Spirit you mortify the deeds of the flesh, you shall live. For whosoever are led by the Spirit of God, they are the sons of God." [Romans 8:13/14]

"Know you not, that you are the temple of God, and that the Spirit of God dwelleth in you? ....Or know you not, that your members are the temple of the Holy Ghost, who is in you, whom you have from God; and you are not of your own? For you are bought with a great price. Glorify and bear God in your body." [1 Cor. 3:16 and 6:19/20]

"For the flesh lusteth against the Spirit: and the spirit against the flesh; for these are contrary one to another: so that you do not the things that you would. .... And they that are Christ's, have crucified their flesh, with the vices and concupiscences. If we live in the Spirit, let us also walk in the Spirit." [Galatians 5:17,24,25]

"Be angry and sin not. Let not the sun go down upon your anger." [Ephesians 4:26]

In the quotes from the Epistles of St. Paul, he describes the struggle to purify our lower nature. In the first Epistle, I understand that the words 'you shall die' and 'you shall live' refer not much to the body but to the soul and its three higher faculties of the Understanding, the Will, and the Memory. The second Epistle contains explicit statements that we are indeed created in the image of God. The third Epistle describes the utter irreconcilability between living one's life according to the values of the world, as opposed to striving to overcome the lower part of our nature and developing our higher faculties. The fourth Epistle tells us that if we have cause to be angry, we should not lose our self-control. That this is a very difficult thing to do, I know from personal experience. We even commit a fault when we become angry or indignant over the faults of others. Developing our spirituality along these lines will involve a terrible, inner struggle, but the spiritual profit we shall reap will more than compensate for the effort we make.

Our Lord well knows this, for in Matthew 7:13/14, He said:

"Enter ye in at the narrow gate: for wide is the gate, and broad is the way that leadeth to destruction, and how many there are who go in thereat. How narrow is the gate, and strait is the way that leadeth to life: and few there are that find it!"

This inner struggle is also well described in the following verse from Ecclesiasticus:

"Son, when thou comest to the service of God, stand in justice and in fear, and prepare thy soul for temptation." [Ecclesiasticus 2:1]

We come into the service of God when we enter upon the spiritual road. However, we should be confident that we do not travel it alone. Jesus is always with us even though we are not aware of His presence and His help, for did He not tell us that:

"Behold, I am with you all days, even to the consummation of the world." [Matthew 28:20]

After considering these quotations from Scripture, we should ask ourselves how much time we put in for personal prayer. Do we sacrifice a portion of our sleep for this purpose? Do we discipline the palate, in that we eat to live and not live to eat? Attending Mass and saying a few prayers while at Church is laudable, but can hardly be called sacrificial. Some may think that if they go to Mass regularly, and observe the other precepts of the Catholic faith, then that is enough. But some honest observation will show that these acts by themselves do not produce a spiritually vibrant soul. As the saints have pointed out, we benefit from the Mass and the reception of the Eucharist according to our own spiritual disposition, no more and no less. The purpose of this essay is to try to understand what is meant by the word 'Disposition', and as we have seen, it means a never-ending struggle to master our lower nature, to be the 'Overcomer' referred to by our Lord in the Apocalypse of St. John, wherein He tells us that:

> "To him that overcometh, I will give to eat of the tree of life, which is in the paradise of my God. .... He that shall overcome, shall not be hurt by the second death. ..... To him that overcometh, I will give the hidden manna and will give him a white counter, and in the counter, a new name written, which no man knoweth but he that receiveth it. .... He that shall overcome, I will make him a pillar in the temple of my God; and he shall go out no more. .... To him that shall overcome, I will give to sit with me in my throne: as I also have overcome, and am set down with my Father in His throne. .... He that shall overcome shall possess these things. And I will be his God; and he shall be my son." [Apocalypse: 2:7; 2:11; 2:17; 3:12; 3:21; 21:7]

These six quotations of the soul being the 'Overcomer' show the wonderful destiny that our Lord intends for us if we never give up the struggle to overcome our lower nature. He tells us this because we are 'made in the image of God' [Genesis 1:27], but unless we challenge ourselves to do more, the timepiece of our souls will do no more than tick over. It is not necessary to practise extraordinary penances, but to try to take advantage of those daily opportunities we have to practise self-restraint in every aspect of our lives. There is no lack of such situations in which we can practise self-restraint.

I should now like to quote a very powerful passage from the Spiritual Canticle, by St. John of the Cross. Near the completion of this work, St. John of the Cross laments the loss of our opportunity to make spiritual progress, to gain some understanding that we are created in the image of God, to be the Overcomer desired of us by our Lord, when he breaks forth in the following beautiful and impassioned appeal to souls:

"O souls created for these grandeurs and called thereto! What do you do? Wherein do ye occupy yourselves? Your desires are meannesses, and your possessions miseries. O wretched blindness of the eyes of your souls, which are blind to so great a light and deaf to so clear a voice, seeing not that for so long as ye seek grandeurs and glories ye remain miserable and mean, and have become ignorant and unworthy of so many blessings!"

St. John of the Cross makes this appeal, because he has experienced the reality of the words of Genesis: 1:27: "And God created man to his own image: to the image of God, he created him…." This means that the very image of the Trinity is implanted in the most secret place of our soul. It is the great destiny of man that he is the only creature who has been given the opportunity to consciously realise this image of God within, and in the words of St. John of the Cross and other saints, to become 'God by participation'. But we squander this opportunity to make spiritual progress during our lifetime on trivialities. He knows, as do all the saints, that the struggle to overcome our lower nature must be constant and unremitting.

St. Paul tells us what our spiritual destiny is in Romans 8: 14/17:

"For whosoever are led by the Spirit of God, they are the sons of God. For you have not received the spirit of bondage again in fear; but you have received the spirit of adoption of sons, whereby we cry: Abba (Father). For the Spirit himself giveth testimony to our spirit, that we are the sons of God. And if sons, heirs also; heirs indeed of God, and joint heirs with Christ: yet so, if we suffer with him, that we may be also glorified with Him."

There are no half-measures in the spiritual life, for we cannot compromise with God. We have nothing to lose by making every effort that lies in our power to make spiritual progress, and this we should do, for as St. John of the Cross warns us in his famous ascetical and mystical work, the Ascent of Mount Carmel:

> "It is greatly to be lamented that, when God has granted them [i.e. souls] strength to break other and stouter cords - namely, affections for sins and vanities - they should fail to attain to such blessing [i.e. virtues and favours granted by God] because they have not shaken off some childish thing which God has bidden them conquer for love of Him, and which is nothing more than a thread or a hair. And what is worse, not only do they make no progress, but because of this attachment they fall back, lose that which they have gained, and retrace that part of the road along which they have travelled at the cost of so much time and labour; for it is well known that, on this road, not to go forward is to turn back, and not to be gaining is to be losing. This our Lord desired to teach us when He said: 'He that is not with Me is against Me; and he that gathereth not with Me scattereth.'" [Matthew 12:30]

Prayer – Its Necessity and its Difficulties

In one of the Sunday Bulletins in a Church in England, we were told that:

> "Praying should be the most natural thing in the world. God didn't just make us and then walk off and leave us to it. He continually holds us in being, sustaining us every minute of the day. The life we live, every breath, every movement, is possible only because God continues to hold us, filling us with His Spirit and breathing life into us. God is closer to us than we can ever imagine - He has built into us an intimacy with Him that is quite astonishing. We are already filled with God; we are already part of God. The natural expression of this bond between us and God is prayer. Prayer is our depths speaking to the depths of God. Through prayer we can share our joys and our sadness, finding refreshment and peace."

The question then arises, why do we find prayer so difficult if it should be natural to our being in relation to God's Being? The answer lies mostly in our will, and the attention, which is directed by our will. Because we are in the body, which is in the world, our attention is continually dragged hither and thither, and our will, which seeks satisfaction through the outward expressions and enjoyments of the mind, finds prayer to God distasteful, since God can only be known within that deepest part of us wherein He resides. Most of us find it very difficult to 'interiorise', to find that centre of our being, because of the distractions of the mind which always intervene. Most of us usually begin our prayer life with the type of prayer which gives us satisfaction, and which occupies the mind, such as vocal prayer or discursive meditation. But the saints tell us that to truly progress, we must go beyond these types of prayer to what is termed the prayer of recollection, silent prayer, or contemplative prayer. We are then led onward by God Himself. We shall have more to say on the types of prayer below.

It is then natural to ask ourselves, what will this discipline, this giving up of many of the 'good things of life' give us in return? The answer to that question can perhaps be put this way. If we wish to create an agreement between two things, in this case, the soul and God, we must put into place a correspondence or conformity between them. Prayer combined with mortification creates this condition. St. John of the Cross, in Stanza III of his Spiritual Canticle, put the matter succinctly when he said:

> "…. Wherefore the soul, remembering here the saying of the Beloved which runs 'Seek and you shall find', determines to go forth herself…. to seek Him in very deed, and not to rest until she finds Him as do many who desire not that God shall cost them more than words, and even those badly put together, and will scarcely do anything for Him if it cost them anything. And some, for His sake, would not even rise from a place which is to their pleasure and liking unless by their doing so the sweetness of God came to their mouths

and hearts without their moving a step and mortifying themselves by losing any of their useless desires, consolations and pleasures. But until they leave these in order to seek Him, they will not find Him, no matter how much they cry to Him; for thus did the Bride seek Him in the Songs and found Him not until she went forth to seek Him. …. And after passing through certain trials, she says here that she found Him."

We should also consider who it is that we seek to find. It is nothing less than our Creator, the ineffable Being who brought forth the physical universe, of which even man's science has but an imperfect knowledge, what to speak of the spiritual heavens of which we know little or nothing. As St. Paul put it:

"That eye hath not seen, nor ear heard, neither hath it entered into the heart of man, what things God hath prepared for them that love him." [1 Cor 2:9]

And yet St. Paul did have his own experience, for he tells us that:

"I know a man in Christ above fourteen years ago (whether in the body, I know not, or out of the body, I know not: God knoweth), such a one caught up to the third heaven. And I know such a man (whether in the body, or out of the body, I know not: God knoweth): That he was caught up into paradise, and heard secret words, which it is not granted to man to utter." [2 Cor 12:2/4].

The Three Kinds of Prayer

Vocal Prayer raises our minds to God and helps to create an atmosphere of receptivity to His Presence within us. The most common difficulty with vocal prayer is that, although the tongue and the lips recite vocal prayers, the mind is far away, thinking of other things. St. Teresa of Avila described this difficulty in her work 'The Way of Perfection', where she tells us that: "…... It is impossible to speak to God and to the world at the same time; yet this is just what we are trying to do when we are saying our prayers and at the same time listening to the conversation of others or letting our thoughts wander on any matter that occurs to us, without making an effort to control them."

In Volume One of The Three Ages of the Interior Life, Fr. Garrigou-Lagrange describes the vocal prayer said without any intention of what we are praying as 'Deformed Psalmody', which, he says: "…. is a body without a soul. Generally, it is marked by unseemly haste, as if undue haste, which, according to St. Francis de Sales, is the death of devotion, could replace true and profound life. …. As a result of haste, the psalmody of which we are speaking is mechanical and not organic; just as in a body without a soul. …. The higher faculties do not live in a prayer made thus; they remain somnolent or scattered." Although Fr. Garrigou-Lagrange is speaking about the recitation of the Office, which is an obligation of priests and other religious, it is nevertheless applicable to all of us who recite vocal prayer in the manner described by him. For example, in Volume Two of The Three Ages of the Interior Life, Fr. Garrigou-Lagrange tells us that in order to attain to the spiritual aspects inherent in the prayer of the Rosary, which contains the infinite merits of Christ, then the Rosary "is no longer the mechanical recitation of the Hail Mary, but a living thing, a school of contemplation." St. Teresa of Avila said essentially the same thing in regard to the recitation of the Paternoster, that is, the 'Our Father'.

Mental Prayer is, for example, meditating on one of the mysteries of the Rosary, or on a passage from Scripture, and reflecting on it, or on something that we have read in a good spiritual book. This awakens higher emotions, which operate to arouse the soul to greater devotion. In speaking of this type of prayer, St. Teresa tells us that even vocal prayer must be accompanied by meditation: "…...for if a person does not think whom he is addressing, and what he is asking for, and who it is that is asking, and of whom he is asking it, I do not consider that he is praying at all even though he be constantly moving his lips. ….."

The great advantage of mental prayer over vocal prayer is that it fixes the attention on the subject matter of the prayer, be it the Rosary, a passage of Scripture, or even a loving conversation with God. If the mind wanders, which it undoubtedly will, since that is its nature, then we simply bring it back again to the subject of our prayer. In the Introduction to the Devout Life, St. Francis de Sales describes ten meditations which could form the subject of one's mental prayer.

Contemplative Prayer (also known as 'The Prayer of Recollection')
In Volume Two of The Three Ages of the Interior Life, Fr. Garrigou-Lagrange tells us that: "What the great spiritual writers tell us about contemplative prayer is within the reach of the interior soul if it is willing to follow the way of humility and abnegation, and if it daily grasps a little better the following verse from the Magnificat: "He hath put down the mighty from their seat, and hath exalted the humble." This Magnificat said by the Blessed Mother to Elizabeth in Luke, chapter 1 puts us in mind of the verse from Isaias 40:4 "Every valley shall be exalted, and every mountain and hill shall be made low, and the crooked shall become straight, and the rough ways plain."

In his Manual for Interior Souls, Fr. Grou describes contemplative prayer as: "The prayer of the heart, which consists of an habitual and constant disposition of love to God …… This disposition of the heart is that in which all Christians ought to be; it was the disposition of all the saints, and it is in it alone that the interior life consists …... God calls all the world to this disposition of heart, for it is without contradiction to all Christians that Jesus Christ addressed Himself when he said that we must always pray……"

In the Dark Night of the Soul, which is the continuation and conclusion of the Ascent of Mount Carmel, St. John of the Cross describes contemplation as "…. naught less than a secret, peaceful and loving infusion from God, which, if it be permitted, enkindles the soul with the spirit of love…....". In the Third Spiritual Alphabet, Francisco Osuna tells us that "…....this devotion recollects sensuality, which previously had run about in a disorderly and unsubmissive way, and places it under the jurisdiction of reason. …. (it) recollects the powers of the soul with the soul's highest part where the image of God is imprinted. ….. You should also remember that no one masters any art without arduous practice, and the more one practises and becomes accustomed to something, the more quickly he masters it. … If you sincerely wish to be a student of recollection, you must commit yourself totally, or not at all. ….. good theology teaches that the more spiritual is prayer, the more meritorious and acceptable to God it is since it requires greater faith and hope." Osuna also tells us that: "The purpose of humility corresponds to that of recollection, for in both we are to become emptied of ourselves so that our hearts may be filled more with God."

Francisco Osuna also said, in a reference to Matthew 12:30, that when we devote time to the prayer of recollection or silent prayer, this exercise gathers us and our desires into ourselves, so that instead of scattering, we are gathering, that is, we are recollecting ourselves, restraining our thoughts from wandering here, there and everywhere. In the same work, he states that: "If the religious would like to know how harmful vocal prayer is to those who wish to devote themselves to contemplation, they should read the first treatise by Rosetto, which speaks of prayer; then they will realise that vocal prayer is of little use and is greatly harmful to the proficient because it can obstruct much greater perfection." Also: "You should intimately quiet your mind and still your understanding, allowing nothing whatsoever to enter, nor should you even speak loving words when you begin to feel communion with the Lord, though they may seem good and your soul may take pleasure in them. For it is better to be totally attentive to recollecting yourself and perfecting yourself in it…..."

In the Ascent of Mount Carmel St. John of the Cross makes it abundantly clear that even discursive meditation or mental prayer can be a blockage to further spiritual progress, when he tells us that:

"Great, therefore, is the error of many spiritual persons who have practised approaching God by means of images and forms and meditations, as befits beginners. God would now lead them on to further spiritual blessings, which are interior and invisible, by taking from them the pleasure and sweetness of discursive meditation; but they cannot, or dare not, or know not how to detach themselves from those palpable methods to which they have grown accustomed….. For the farther the soul progresses in spirituality, the more it ceases from the operation of the faculties in particular acts since it becomes more and more occupied in one act that is general and pure; and thus the faculties that were journeying to a place where the soul has arrived cease to work, even as the feet stop and cease to move when the journey is over."

Since it is very important for a person to know when to cease from mental prayer, St. John of the Cross gives three signs:

"…. whereby he may know whether or not it will be meet for him to lay them aside at this season. This first sign is his realization that he can no longer meditate or reason with his imagination, neither can take pleasure therein as he was wont to do aforetime; he rather finds aridity in that which aforetime was wont to captivate his senses and to bring him sweetness. But, for as long as he finds sweetness in meditation, and is able to reason, he should not abandon this, save when his soul is led into the peace and quietness which is described under the third head. The second sign is a realization that he has no desire to fix his meditation or his sense upon other particular objects, exterior or interior. I do not mean that the imagination neither comes nor goes (for even at times of deep recollection it is apt to move freely), but that the soul has no pleasure in fixing it of set purpose upon other objects. The third and surest sign is that the soul takes pleasure in being alone, and waits with loving attentiveness upon God, without making any particular meditation, in inward peace and quietness at rest, and without acts and exercises of the faculties - memory, understanding and will - at least, without discursive acts, that is, without passing from one thing to another; the soul is alone, with attentiveness and a knowledge, general and loving, as we have said, but without any particular understanding, and adverting not to that which it is contemplating.

"These three signs, at least, the spiritual person must observe in himself, all together, before he can venture safely to abandon the state of meditation and sense, and to enter that of contemplation and spirit. And it suffices not for a man to have the first alone without the second, for it might be that the reason for his being unable to imagine and meditate upon the things of God, as he did aforetime, was distraction on his part and lack of diligence, for the which cause he must observe in himself the second likewise, which is the absence of inclination or desire to think upon other things; for when the inability to fix the imagination and sense upon the things of God proceeds from distraction and lukewarmness, the soul then has the desire and inclination to fix it upon other and different things, which lead it thence altogether. Neither does it suffice that he should observe in himself the first and second signs, if he observes not likewise, together with these, the third; for, although he observes his inability to reason and think upon the things of God, and likewise his distaste for thinking upon other and different things, this might proceed from melancholy or from some other kind of humour in the brain or the heart, which habitually produces a certain absorption and suspension of the senses, causing the soul to think not at all, nor to desire or be inclined to think, but rather to remain in that pleasant state of reverie. Against this must be set the third sign, which is loving attentiveness and knowledge, in peace, etc., as we have said."

The following extract taken from the Catechism of the Catholic Church on contemplative prayer is also instructive:

2711 Entering into contemplative prayer is like entering into the Eucharistic liturgy: we "gather up" the heart, recollect our whole being under the prompting of the Holy Spirit, abide in the dwelling place of the Lord which we are, awaken our faith in order to enter into the presence of Him Who awaits us. We let our masks fall and turn our hearts back to the Lord who loves us, so as to hand ourselves over to Him as an offering to be purified and transformed.

So, it can be understood from the subject matter taken from the writings quoted above, that it is during the time that we practise contemplative prayer that God infuses Himself into our soul, quite unknown to us, even when it seems we are achieving nothing, and that all we are conscious of is the spate of unwanted thoughts and dryness in our prayer. It is this unconscious infusion that is the major benefit of contemplative prayer.

Therefore, it is important to understand that, when we are waiting upon God in silent prayer, we are doing something far greater than we can realise. We may not experience that Divine calm and peace, together with a wondrous and sublime knowledge of God, that is spoken of below in the quote from the Ascent of Mount Carmel by St. John of the Cross, but we are achieving more than we realise, not only for ourselves, but for other souls, when we attempt to unite ourselves with God within. As Fr. Grou put it in his Manual for Interior Souls when speaking of certain temptations:

"This happens above all with regard to prayer, when we have no longer good thoughts and affections, and when we are assailed with distractions. Then we immediately think we are doing nothing, and we are tempted to give up our way of prayer and return to ordinary meditation. This is a delusion which we must fight against strenuously. Prayer is the death of self-love, and it is never more effective for producing this death than it is when it is dry, distracted, and without any consolation or sensible devotion."

The most common difficulty in contemplative prayer is that the mind easily tires of practising the loving attentiveness to the presence of God within us. And as with vocal prayer, where, although the tongue and the lips are uttering words, the mind is off somewhere else, so it is with the practice of contemplative prayer. We may look as though we are deeply engrossed in prayer, but if we do not strive to keep the attention fixed on this loving attentiveness, the mind will drift away and be caught up in extraneous thoughts and various imaginings, whether due to the activities of our day, or in the past, and also as a result of our interactions with others, good or bad. We may look very holy to others, but all we do is to fool ourselves if we do not constantly strive to bring back the attention of our mind to what we should be about. Because it is important to note that, after discerning the three signs within us as explained by St. John of the Cross, and we enter upon the practice of contemplative prayer, we are taking on the work of a lifetime.

The question may arise as to whether a soul that begins to practise contemplative prayer should sometimes return to mental prayer, at least for a while. St. John of the Cross addresses this question in the Ascent of Mount Carmel, when he says:

"With regard to that which has been said, there might be raised one question - if progressives (that is, those whom God is beginning to bring into this supernatural knowledge of contemplation, whereof we have spoken) must never again, because of this that they are beginning to experience, return to the way of meditation and reasoning and natural forms. To this the answer is that it is not to be understood that such as are beginning to experience this loving knowledge must, as a general rule, never again try to return to meditation; for, when they are first making progress in proficiency, the habit of contemplation is not yet so perfect that they can give themselves to the act thereof whensoever they wish, nor, in the same way, have they reached a point so far beyond meditation that they cannot occasionally meditate and reason in a natural way, as they were wont, using the figures and the steps that they were wont to use, and finding something new in them. Rather, in these early stages, when, by means of the indications already given, they are able to see that the soul is not occupied in that repose and knowledge, they will need to make use of meditation until by means of it they come to acquire in some degree of perfection the habit which we have described. This will happen when, as soon as they seek to meditate, they experience this knowledge and peace, and find themselves unable to meditate and no longer desirous of doing so, as we have said. For until they reach this stage, which is that of the proficient in this exercise, they use sometimes one and sometimes the other, at different times. ……"

"When the spiritual person cannot meditate, let him learn to be still in God, fixing his loving attention upon Him, in the calm of his understanding, although he may think himself to be doing nothing. For thus, little by little and very quickly, Divine calm and peace will be infused into his soul, together with wondrous and sublime knowledge of God, enfolded in Divine love. And let him not meddle with forms, meditations and imaginings, or with any kind of reasoning, lest his soul be disturbed, and brought out of its contentment and peace, which can only result in its experiencing distaste and repugnance. And if, as we have said, such a person scruples that he is doing nothing, let him note that he is doing no small thing by pacifying the soul and bringing it into calm and peace, unaccompanied by any act or desire, for it is this that our Lord asks us of us, through David, saying: Vacate, et videte quoniam ego sum Deus. As though he had said: Learn to be empty of all things (that is to say, inwardly and outwardly) and you will see that I am God."

When we find the mind wandering off in our prayer, and we desire to return to mental prayer for a while, a method described under the heading 'Aspirations, Ejaculatory Prayers, and Good Thoughts' is explained by St. Francis de Sales in his work, the Introduction to the Devout life. He tells us:

"We retire into God before we aspire to Him, and we aspire to Him so that we may retire into Him. Hence, aspirations to be with God and spiritual retirement support one another and both proceed and are born from good thoughts. Make spiritual aspirations to God by short, ardent movements of your heart, Philothea. Marvel at His beauty, implore His help, cast yourself in spirit at the foot of the cross, adore his goodness, converse often with Him about your salvation, present your soul to Him a thousand times during the day, fix your interior eyes upon his sweet countenance, stretch out your hand to Him like a child to his father so that he may lead you on, place Him in your bosom like a fragrant bouquet, plant Him in your heart like a flag, and make a thousand motions of your heart to provide you with love of God and arouse in yourself a passionate and tender affection for this Divine Spouse."

But St. Francis does not recommend being burdened by fixed or rote prayers, which are stultifying to the soul, and keep it bound. Rather, he tells us:

"However, my advice is not to restrict yourself to a form of words but to pronounce either within your heart or with your lips such words as love suggests to you at the time. It will supply you with as many as you wish. It is true that there are certain words that have a special power to satisfy the heart in this respect. Such are the aspirations strewn so thickly throughout the Psalms of David, various invocations of the name of Jesus, and the loving thoughts uttered in the Canticle of Canticles….."

When we practise contemplative prayer, we are to bring our attention up to the eye level, which is the focal point of the seat of the higher part of the soul in the body, as explained below under the heading of 'Higher and Lower Parts of the Soul'. With our eyes closed, we surrender the activities of our faculties of the heart and mind, and we await the grace of the Holy Spirit to descend upon us, giving us the peace of His communion with our soul. This is to find the little alter within, although it is not so much as finding it, but of resting within it. The heart of the soul is the interior tabernacle, and the initial impulse comes from God; it is Love itself that calls us. Our task is to come before Him in prayer and devotion, and He will draw us to the tabernacle of the heart. Gently and quietly, we will feel His Presence interiorly.

As St. John tells us in the Apocalypse 3:20:

"Behold I stand at the gate and knock. If any man shall hear my voice, and open to me the door, I will come into him and will sup with him, and he with me."

Here, it may be noted that our attention automatically goes to the eye-centre whenever we are engaged in outer studies or in carrying out some tasks in which we need to focus our attention. But we have little or no experience of directing our attention within at the time of prayer, whether this be vocal, mental, or contemplative prayer. The attention is the power of the soul, and when we focus it within, we are, in the words of Francisco Osuna referred to above, gathering with Christ, and not scattering.

Our Lord gave very few instructions on how to pray, but when He did so, it was contemplative prayer or the prayer of recollection that he described in Matthew 6:6:

> "But when thou shalt pray, enter thy chamber, and having shut the door, pray to thy Father in secret, and thy Father who seeth in secret will repay thee."

And in Psalm 45:11:

> "Be still and see that I am God; I will be exalted among the nations, and I will be exalted in the earth."

The reward for watching, that is, persevering in our prayer no matter how difficult it is and if we are also left without consolation, is set out in Matthew 24: 46/47:

> "Blessed is that servant, whom when his lord shall come, he shall find so doing. Amen I say to you, he shall place him over all his goods."

In Matthew, Chapter 25, the parable of the ten virgins, five of whom were foolish, because they did not take oil for their lamps with them, whereas the five wise virgins did take oil in their vessels for their lamps, also speaks to us of not giving up prayer, no matter what the circumstances are, or how discouraged we might sometimes become.

Higher and Lower Parts of the Soul

The great spiritual teachers who are also great mystics, such as St. John of the Cross and St. Teresa of Avila, tell us that there are two parts of the soul, the higher part and the lower part. The higher part contains the spirit (the image of God within us), and the three faculties of the soul, which are the understanding, the will, and the memory. The lower part contains the passions, emotions, and desires. St. John of the Cross tells us that when these are unbridled, there arise in the soul all the vices and imperfections, and when they are ordered, all the virtues. When the passions are unrestrained, they result in the seven capital sins already referred to. In The Three Ages of the Interior Life - Volume One, Fr. Garrigou–Lagrange tells us that the great scholastic theologian, St. Thomas Aquinas, said: "These sins spring from inordinate self–love, or egoism, which hinders us from loving God above all else and incline us to turn away from Him." Fr. Garrigou–Lagrange further explains that: "the capital sins are so called, because they are like the head or the principle of many others. We are, first of all, inclined toward them, and by them in turn toward sins that are often more serious."

Let us again recall that St. John of the Cross tells us that while these sins result in "all the imperfections and disorders of the sensual [or lower part of the soul], they have their strength and root in the spirit, where all habits, both good and bad, are brought into subjection, and thus until these are purged, the rebellions and depravities of sense cannot be purged thoroughly." Consequently, not only are they the source of our troubles in life, they also hold the higher part of the soul captive. When we commence to discipline our passions, emotions and desires, it is then that we take our first step in the spiritual life of developing the necessary dispositions for prayer, and we begin to loosen the hold that these sins have on the higher part of the soul. Referring again to the First Epistle of St. John, wherein he describes the passions, emotions and desires as the 'concupiscence of the flesh, the concupiscence of the eyes, and the pride of life', the word 'concupiscence' simply means 'unbridled or uncontrolled desire'. When we enter with a firm resolve upon the spiritual life, we begin the onerous task of purging or cleansing the lower part of the soul from these vices, and we also begin to create the dispositions necessary for prayer. God also takes a hand in this work, for without His help, we could not accomplish this task, especially as it relates to cleansing the higher part of the soul, and this participation of God is described Ecclesiasticus 2:1 and 2:5, wherein we are told:

> "Son, when thou comest to the service of God, stand in justice and in fear, and prepare thy soul for temptation. For gold and silver are tried in the fire, but acceptable men in the furnace of humiliation."

God's work in this cleansing is also described in Proverbs 3:12:

> "My son, reject not the correction of the Lord: and do not faint when thou art chastised by Him: For whom the Lord loveth, he chastiseth: and as a father in the son, he pleaseth himself."

So it can be seen that when we enter upon the work of creating the necessary dispositions for prayer in order to participate with God in the cleansing of the higher and lower parts of our soul, we are actually entering into the service of God.

In Volume One of The Three Ages of the Interior Life, Fr. Garrigou-Lagrange tells us that:

> "If we carefully consider the human soul in its nature, we see two quite different regions in it: one belongs to the sensible order, the other to the suprasensible or intellectual order. The sensitive part of the soul is that which is common to men and animals; it includes the external senses and the internal senses, comprising the imagination, the sensible memory, and also sensibility, or the sensitive appetite, whence spring the various passions or emotions, which we call sensible love and hatred, desire and aversion, sensible joy and sadness, hope and despair, audacity and fear, and anger. All this sensitive life exists in the animal, whether its passions are mild like

those of the dove or the lamb, or whether they are strong like those of the wolf and the lion. Above this sensitive part common to men and animals, our nature likewise possesses an intellectual part, which is common to men and angels, although it is far more vigorous and beautiful in the angel. By this intellectual part our soul towers above our body; this is why we say that the soul is spiritual, that it does not intrinsically depend on the body and will thus be able to survive the body after death. From the essence of the soul in this elevated region spring our two higher faculties, the intellect, and the will...."

Fr. Garrigou-Lagrange also tells us that:

"The Holy Ghost is the soul of the mystical body, of which Christ is the head. As in our body, the soul is entirely in the whole body and entirely in each part, and exercises its superior functions in the head, so the Holy Ghost is entirely in the mystical body, entirely in each just soul, and exercises His highest functions in the holy soul of the Saviour, and through it on us...... Only in all the mystical life does the soul truly awaken completely, and have that lively, profound, radiating consciousness of the gift of God that is necessary if the soul is to correspond fully with the love of God for us."

So, if we wish to experience our true nature and identity as described herein, it is necessary to develop within ourselves the right dispositions, aided by the practice of the virtues. This, when combined with the persevering practice of prayer, will help us to make as much progress as we can in this short life before our lease runs out at the time of our death, after which we can no longer merit.

SOME THOUGHTS ON FREE WILL

Perhaps we can define free will as the choice we make when we are faced with choosing between more than one alternative, whatever they may be. In most cases, we find little difficulty in this, because we usually choose what pleases us. Sometimes, we delude ourselves that what pleases us pleases God also. But we should ask ourselves the question: 'How free is our will when we choose?' Upon reflection, we may be shocked to find that our so-called free will is not free at all, because it is not a disinterested act of choice that we make. Take the simple example of a person who buys a chocolate bar. How many persons have we run across who declare quite honestly that once they have bitten into it, they usually finish off the whole bar rather than say, taking three or four pieces and putting the rest aside for another day. Now, the act of buying the chocolate bar is what one would call an act of free will, but it is really an act of self-will, which is motivated by the desire for a piece of chocolate, and if we end up eating the whole bar we are dictated to by the sense of taste. I am not for one moment suggesting that we should stop eating chocolate bars; that isn't the point at all. I am merely pointing out that most of our acts (and thoughts) have their source in a particular desire or act of self-will, which can so dominate us that we think that we are free agents, but are really subject to lower desires or emotions. Consider also how many souls are bound by alcohol, drugs, and many other addictions. These addictions started out by a deliberate choice, what the person who made it would call an act of free will, and which thereafter led to bondage. Things become even more difficult when we have to make moral or ethical choices. Our free will is then conditioned by the nature of the situation we face, and if we have any personal interest in any particular outcome, then this difficulty in exercising true free will greatly increases. Let us see what two saints have to say about it. St. Vincent de Paul, the Founder of the Congregation of the Mission and of the Sisters of Charity, tells us that:

"Self-will is what spoils and corrupts our devotions, labours and penances. Therefore, not to lose time and trouble, we must endeavor never to act from the impulse of nature, interest, inclination, temper or caprice, but always from the pure and simple motive of doing the will of God, and accustom ourselves to this in all things…..."

St. Catherine of Genoa tells us that:

"There is no pest more malignant than that of self-will, which is so subtle, so malicious, so deeply seated, which conceals itself in so many ways and defends itself by so many reasons, that it seems indeed a demon….. When it cannot gain direct obedience, it knows well how to win its way in some other form and under various excuses and pretexts…... we are all the while seeking, contriving and cherishing our own interests. I behold in it a sea of malice so envenomed, so opposed to God, that He alone can rescue us from it, and since He sees this better than we, He has great compassion on us and never ceases to send us inspirations, contradictions, and helps of all sorts to deliver us."

'But', you will say, 'God gave us free will, and if you are telling us that we really don't have it, then this free will is a bit of an illusion.' But if self-will masquerades under free will, it is true that our so-called free will is an illusion. We can only exercise true free will when our will is in accord with God's will. Therefore, we must do our part, and we do this when we begin to set our own house (i.e. our senses and emotions) in order, and to make some effort to correspond our will with that of God's Will, because when two things correspond one to the other, there is a sort of equality between them.

Two virtues which today's society has little use for are humility and purity, but both of these are essential if we wish to achieve progress towards this equality which will make us friends of God. They are most effectively developed in our youth, for it is false philosophy to tell ourselves that God can wait because our first priority is to enjoy life to the full. The value of curtailing our passions and desires when we are young is that we are then making God an acceptable offering. It is not acceptable to Him if we live a worldly life, and then in our middle age, when we have exhausted most of our passions and energies to say that: 'Now, God, we will give some time to You.' Any reasonable person who is offered a gift of something second or third hand would not be pleased with it; similarly, it is no gift to God to offer Him a worn-out shell. And if we consider the matter, if we offer God our best in our youth, are we not offering Him something which we first received from Him as a free gift!

The saints achieved their sanctity by asking themselves in virtually every act they made whether it would please God. St. Peter Julian Eymard, the Founder of the Blessed Sacrament Fathers, when preaching to members of his congregation, told them that there are three degrees of the purity of love:

> "The first degree is to want no sensual satisfaction away from God. The second degree is to share every honest and good satisfaction with our Lord, which is more perfect. The third degree is to be indifferent to the various states through which God wants us to pass, be they joyous or sad, and in case of a choice, it is generosity in always choosing the most difficult, the most crucifying, because that is what Jesus Christ did Himself."

Admittedly, the saint is preaching to members of his congregation, who are consecrated religious, but the key he offers us is to do everything with reference to the glory of God, even a simple thing like eating. This is why we should say grace before our meal, whether in words or mentally, since we are giving thanks to God. At the same time, we will become conscious of the need to practise a little more discipline, a little more mortification, in all our activities. We may not attain to the height that the saints achieved in these disciplines, and God may not expect this of us, living so much in the world as we do, but surely we can do something. In his Introduction to the Devout Life, St. Francis de Sales tells us:

> "You should also read stories and lives of the saints for there, as in a mirror, you can see a picture of the Christian life and adapt their deeds to your use in keeping with your vocation. Acts of the saints cannot be strictly imitated by people living in the world, yet they can be followed either closely or from a distance."

The will is a good servant but a bad master, since perverse acts of the will poison the intellect. When we commit serious sin by allowing the passions and appetites to exert control over us, the will is weakened; one might say that deep furrows are forged in the will which permit the seeds of sin and perverse behaviour to take root in us, and once the will is weakened, it is extremely difficult to exert it in order to resist those things, both outer and inner, which result in the power of understanding from becoming further clouded, and we eventually have no power to resist the attractions of the appetites of the flesh. However, our Lord provided the remedy for this in the Sacrament of Reconciliation, and it is my understanding that if we approach the Sacrament in the right spirit and with a firm intention to amend our faults, then Our Lord will restore the integrity of our will, but we must cooperate with this grace, otherwise it will not be effective. We cooperate with this grace by avoiding those occasions where we are likely to transgress, to fall into immoral behaviour, and also by recalling those situations in which we know that we fell from grace so that we do not repeat past mistakes. And in order to maintain the integrity of our free will, we must practise the two virtues of temperance and fortitude.

Today, our outer senses are assaulted by a myriad of foul images and words from television and other communication media much more than has been the case in past decades. Therefore, we must be more vigilant than ever to maintain the integrity of our free will. No one can do this work for us; God will help and extend His grace, but we must cooperate with that grace. If we choose not to, then we cannot presume that God will force His will upon us. Saints and those theologians who write on mystical theology tell us that the higher faculties of the soul (those which survive death) consist of the memory, will and intellect. Some of them dispute which is the noblest of these faculties, the intellect or the will. We don't have to trouble ourselves about this. The one thing that we have to realise is that although our intellect receives its light from the Divine Intellect, we can impede this light if we allow our free will to become corrupted by serious sin. And if this process continues, we can descend lower in nature than the animals.

The saints sometimes suffered grievous temptations, but the difference between such temptations and those we are subject to is that God often allows His saints to be tried in order to develop the will and the virtues in them to a heroic degree, while more often than not, we succumb to our temptations or even go out of our way to seek them.

Some people will say that they 'see nothing wrong' in doing what we know is wrong, and they can give a hundred and one reasons for saying this; we can see examples of this sort of thing on television or read about it in the newspapers. We can only conclude about such people that they have killed their conscience, that warning voice of God within, and it will require much prayer on the part of their friends (if indeed such persons have such generous and true friends) to bring about a radical change in behaviour. We must flee at once from such people or such situations. Our Lord spoke of this in Matthew 5:29/30, where He counsels us in the following powerful and symbolic language:

> "And if thy right eye scandalize thee, pluck it out and cast it from thee. For it is expedient for thee that one of thy members should perish, rather than that thy whole body be cast into hell. And if thy right hand scandalize thee, cut it off, and cast it from thee: For it is

expedient for thee that one of thy members should perish, rather than that thy whole body go into hell."

Our Lord repeats these words, with minor variation, in Matthew 18:8/9. Clearly, the meaning of these passages is that we must flee all occasions of sin lest we irretrievably impair the higher faculties of the soul. I believe that maintaining the integrity of our will is key to this, and while we may always avail ourselves of the saving Sacrament of Reconciliation to restore its integrity, we should not underestimate the value of our own efforts.

ON THE WILL OF GOD

In his homily during Sunday morning Mass (on August 19th, 2001) in Poole, England, the priest talked about the precarious state of the priesthood, in that vocations to the priesthood in Britain were at dangerously low levels, and he asked all parishioners to pray for this purpose. He specifically pointed out the need for young men to answer this calling, since only they could identify with and provide the example and leadership for the youth of today, and that they, not the older generations, possessed the necessary vigour and energy which the task of directing youth required. He also mentioned that youth would be more likely to accept discipline from someone of their own generation than from those their senior in years. The priest then identified youth clubs led by priests as probably the best vehicle for this purpose. He went on to describe the vocation to the priesthood as a sacrifice of self for others, and as a passive form of suffering. He went on to explain that the word 'passive', when referred back to the Latin from which it was derived, means 'to suffer'.

I am not here concerned with whether or not being an effective leader of youth clubs is the best qualification for a person considering a vocation to the priesthood, but with two examples the priest gave from his own ministry on his experience of passive suffering. The first example concerned a young mother of four children who lost three of them in a house fire. He described how, when he went to the hospital where the mother and surviving child were recovering, he found her comforting this child, and how stoic she was in 'accepting the will of God'. In the second example, he went to comfort the mother of an only child, a girl of eighteen, who was killed in an automobile accident not far from her home while travelling in her mini-car to commence studies at university. What had happened was that a large cement truck travelling in the opposite direction got out of control, crashed through the barrier separating the two sides of the road, and ran over the mini-car, crushing the poor girl to death. The mother's words to the priest were: 'It must have been the will of God.'

The priest did not tell us what he said on the occasion of each of these two tragedies. I am sure he must have greatly empathized with both mothers in what he termed as 'passive suffering'.

Another tragedy took place just one week after the priest's homily. Two boys (brothers) ventured out onto the mud flats on the Solent (an arm of the sea that flows between Portsmouth on the mainland and the Isle of Wight, U.K.) when the tide was out, and apparently decided to take a short-cut on their way back. The short-cut took them across certain streams of the sea which were still flowing out with the tide. What they did not know was that these streams could sometimes contain deep water, and due to the flow of the tide could be extremely strong. Unfortunately, the boys fell into one of these streams, with the result that the youngest one was drowned even though, when the coastguard was alerted on the mainland, a helicopter was on the scene in five minutes. The will of God? I don't think so. One of the vicissitudes of life, yes. We shall discuss such incidents towards the end of this essay to see if we can glean some meaning from them, and at its conclusion, I shall state a basic principle that we should always bear in mind.

In a sermon given on the Epistle of St. James 1:17, Meister Eckhart (a famous German theologian and mystic of the 13th/14th century), interpreted the words from the Epistle: "The best gift of all and perfection descend from above from the Father of lights". He said: "**. .... that people who abandon themselves to God and seek only his will with all diligence... whatever God gives to such a person is the best....**" A little further on, he tells us: "Now you could perhaps say:" "How do I know whether it is God's will or not?" He answered this question with:

"Know this: If it were not God's will, it would not be happening. You cannot be sick nor can anything at all happen unless it is God's will. And since you then know that it is God's will, you should have so much delight and satisfaction in it that you do not consider any pain as pain. Even if it were the most excruciating of all pain, if you then were to feel any pain or suffering, this would be completely wrong. You should accept it from God as the best thing of all because it must of necessity be the best thing for you. God's being depends upon his [always] willing the best...." [This extract from Meister Eckhart's Sermon was taken from "Meister Eckhart, Teacher and Preacher - The Classics of Western Spirituality - Published by Paulist Press"]

These hard words from Meister Eckhart seem to corroborate the attitude of the two mothers referred to above, in that the tragedy each suffered was 'the will of God'. But this attitude could equally well have been the numbed reaction to a great loss and a moving statement of their faith in God no matter what, because I do not believe that such tragedies necessarily come about as the result of the direct will of God. If we read the words of Meister Eckhart carefully, we will observe that the passage quoted is built upon the words: "...... **that people who abandon themselves to God and seek only his will with all diligence... whatever God gives to such a person is the best....**" Therefore, it seems that the words of Meister Eckhart were not intended to have wide application; but many examples can be found, especially in the lives of the saints (the Book of Job in the Bible illustrates this principle) of God testing the faith of those souls who wish only to do His will.

Although God permits certain terrible events to occur, He does not necessarily will them to happen. There is the widest possible difference between God permitting such events to take place and God willing them to happen. Now, since God is all-powerful, and can certainly prevent evil of any kind from taking place if He so wished, why should this be? Part of the answer lies in the mystery of free will, which we discussed in a previous essay. Can the free will which humanity may exercise actually impinge on God's will to desire the best for His children? I think the answer is 'yes', it can, and this has been the case throughout all human history. In this regard, it is relevant to repeat two quotations given in that essay taken from the writings of St. Vincent de Paul and St Catherine of Genoa:

"Self-will is what spoils and corrupts our devotions, labours and penances. Therefore, not to lose time and trouble, we must endeavor never to act from the impulse of nature, interest, inclination, temper or caprice, but always from the pure and simple motive of doing the will of God, and accustom ourselves to this in all things......"
[St. Vincent de Paul]

"There is no pest more malignant than that of self-will, which is so subtle, so malicious, so deeply seated, which conceals itself in so many ways and defends itself by so many reasons, that it seems indeed a demon..... When it cannot gain direct obedience, it knows well how to win its way in some other form and under various excuses and pretexts....... we are all the while seeking, contriving and cherishing our own interests. I behold in it a sea of malice so envenomed, so opposed to God, that He alone can rescue us from it, and since He sees this better than we, He has great compassion on us and never ceases to send us inspirations, contradictions, and helps of all sorts to deliver us."
[St. Catherine of Genoa]

I think that the quotation from St. Catherine of Genoa clarifies what Meister Eckhart said above, in that God, in his great compassion, never ceases to send us inspirations, contradictions, and helps of all sorts to deliver us. But what if we are not receptive to these inspirations? The inevitable result is that in the great majority of human actions, God's will is not present. Our wills are so selfish, so fragile, so fickle, so unstable, that they rarely, if ever, accord with the will of God. This is why, in the Lord's prayer, Jesus asks us to pray that: 'God's will be done on earth as it is in heaven'. I cannot conceive, and Meister Eckhart would, I believe, be horrified to learn, that we understood his words: **"Know this: If it were not God's will, it would not be happening"** to have application to the great persecutions of religion, and on many occasions, by religion, in the past centuries; to the horrors experienced during the great two great wars of the 20th century, and also those that took place more recently in the Balkan countries. If all such events were the direct result of God's will, this would justify every evil and crime committed by man, and we would be forced to conclude that those committing such heinous offences were but the innocent instruments of God's will instead of being the instruments of evil, which they are. Thus, there would be no justification for punishment at the hand of laws made by man, which is an absurd result. It is for these and similar reasons why I believe Meister Eckhart insisted that we abandon ourselves to God and seek only his will with all diligence before we can say that God's will is behind all that happens in our lives. This is a work of a lifetime, and I believe that we can say that we are making progress when we observe the numerous times when we do our own will, and not the will of God. The more we can identify the selfish motives of our own will behind what we do or say, the less likely are we to repeat our mistakes and the more likely to ask for God's will to be done.

Returning to the tragedies suffered by the two mothers described above, we concluded that their belief that it was the will of God was an act of great faith notwithstanding their great loss and the shock and bewilderment they must have gone through. Another view of such tragedies is that they are not directly willed by God, but occur as one of the innumerable vicissitudes of life, which seem to take the form of blind chance that has no meaning. Personally, I don't believe that such things occur due to blind chance that has no meaning, but while we cannot explain such happenings, I do believe that God always creates good out of evil, and although we rarely see how this comes about, we can, like the two mothers (and as Job in the Bible), make an affirmation of faith to this end.

Although it is not possible to change what has happened, such an affirmation of faith in God has power in it and will undoubtedly help the souls of those who meet their earthly ends in such inexplicable ways, and also sustain those who are left. In this manner, we submit to the will of God without making Him the author of every tragedy of life, many of which occur because of our own negligence or foolhardiness, or because we ignore certain warning signs which, as St Catherine of Genoa tells us, come from God Himself.

Another perspective of the tragedies of life is that we seem to accept certain of these more easily than others. For example, a man or woman in their late sixties or early seventies develops a terminal cancer or other disease. We can often be quite philosophical about this, saying that: 'it is quite sad, of course, but he or she has had a good life and need have few regrets.' Yet when the same thing happens to a young child, we complain bitterly to God saying: 'What a pity it is that such a promising life is cut short before it has begun.' Often, a child is more accepting than an adult of its condition. Indeed, an early death may yield much more spiritual fruit than a long life, a good part of which may have given offence to God, and a rebellious spirit at its end.

I now wish to return to the words of Meister Eckhart on **'people who abandon themselves to God and seek only his will with all diligence'**. If we do this to the best of our ability, we shall attract the protection of God from those so-called chance events, those vicissitudes of life, that are beyond our control, and we shall become more sensitive to those subtle promptings from the spirit of God within us, and what is even better, will become more disposed to listen to them. A life led in this manner will not only redound to our benefit, but will also overflow to our nearest and dearest, subject to their respect for our way of life. This is not to say that we shall sail through life with ease and without suffering, for we too must take up our cross in imitation of Christ, but we shall do so more serenely. And one day, with God's grace, if we conform our will to God's will, we may, like St Paul, be caught up to the third heaven, at which time we shall gain a far greater understanding of Meister Eckhart's words than our present condition will allow. If only a small part of humanity can achieve this conformity of will to God's will, then such will be the overflow of God's grace that we shall be near the time spoken of by the Prophet Isaias, when every tear will be wiped away, and man will offend God no more. Then will our utterance of that part of the Lord's prayer: 'Thy will be done on earth as it is in heaven' be prayed from the heart, and not just by the tongue, and God's will shall then be truly done in our lives.

As a final consideration, I would like to quote from the Gospel according to St. Matthew, chapter 9, verses 16/17 as another example that we cannot understand the words of Scripture in a literal manner. In these verses, our Lord said: **And nobody putteth a piece of raw cloth unto an old garment. For it taketh away the fulness thereof from the garment: and there is made a greater rent. Neither do they put new wine into old bottles. Otherwise the bottles break and the wine runneth out and the bottles perish. But new wine they put into new bottles: and both are preserved.** [Verses 16 and 17 tell us of the rise of Christianity as the Religion to spread the teachings of Jesus throughout the world. Matthew 9:16/17, Luke 5:36/39 and John 10:26 make it clear that the Jewish people as a whole were never intended to embrace Christianity in the time of Jesus. But we have yet to see the end of the story.]

In conclusion, I would like to state a basic principle that helps me to reconcile those occurrences in life which are often beyond our control (and certainly beyond our understanding) with the Will of God. Here, I first refer to the Book of Ecclesiasticus in the Old Testament, and then to the letter of St. Paul to the Romans in the New Testament:

> For all things were known to the Lord God before they were created: so also, after they were perfected, he beholdeth all things. [Chapter 23, verse 29 of the Book of Ecclesiasticus]

For whom he foreknew, he also predestinated to be made conformable to the image of his son: that he might be the firstborn amongst many brethren. And whom he predestinated, them he also called. And whom he called, them he also justified. And whom he justified, them he also glorified. What shall we then say to these things? If God be for us, who is against us? [Chapter 8, verses 29/31 of St. Paul's letter to the Romans]

Thus, from the standpoint of God, everything is "predestined", and this includes all acts arising from the exercise of man's free will. But "predestined" does not mean that the evils resulting from the exercise of man's free will were "foreordained" by God. Otherwise, sin would have no meaning. **There is no correlation between the "foreknowledge" of God and "foreordained".**

FIGHT THE GOOD FIGHT WITH ALL THY MIGHT - CHRIST IS THY STRENGTH AND CHRIST THY LIGHT

This essay is written for those persons who, for one reason or another, or several reasons, have come to the end of their tether, and in consequence, have plumbed the depths of despair, and so feel that there is no way out other than to take their own lives. In the society in which we live today, there is, unfortunately, no lack of well-meaning people who not only condone, but encourage or justify such an extreme measure. Such people have dismissed the teachings of religion in general, do not usually believe that the soul survives the death of the body (if indeed they believe in the existence of the soul at all), or if they do, are convinced that an all-merciful God would forgive and forget. What follows is a response to this attitude of disbelief or misbelief. It is based on a study of Scripture and writings of the saints that spans a period of over fifty years. It is impossible to avoid completely the use of religious terminology, although I will keep it to a minimum, not because I think it should be avoided, but for the reason that it is not the principal intent of writing this essay.

Let us commence with a situation in which we often find ourselves just in the ordinary business of living. We are faced with making a decision in order to solve a particular problem, or to correct a particular error. What we do not do, or do our level best to avoid, is to repeat the same mistake in a different form. This is to jump from the frying pan into the fire. But this is precisely what happens when a person decides to take their own life. They go from one state of despair into a far worse one after having led a life of serious sin. In the book of her life, St. Teresa of Avila graphically describes the state of hell into which an evil soul might find itself. Now, let us beware that the saint is telling us something that she had just imagined she saw. She was a most practical lady, full of common sense as well as a spirituality of the highest order, as a reading of her autobiography will reveal. She writes:

"A long time after the Lord had granted me many of the favours which I have described, together with the other very great ones, I was at prayer one day when suddenly, without knowing how, I found myself, as I thought, plunged right into hell. I realized that it was the Lord's will that I should see the place which the devils had prepared for me there and which I had merited my sins. This happened in the briefest space of time, but, even if I were to live for many years, I believe it would be impossible for me to forget it. The entrance, I thought, resembled a very long, narrow passage, like a furnace, very low, dark and closely confined; the ground seemed to be full of water which looked like filthy, evil-smelling mud, and in it were many wicked-looking reptiles. At the end there was a hollow space scooped out of a wall, like a cupboard, and it was here that I found myself in close confinement. But the sight of all this was pleasant by comparison with what I felt there. What I have said is in no way an exaggeration. My feelings, I think, could not possibly be exaggerated, nor can anyone understand them. I felt a fire within my soul the nature of which I am utterly incapable of describing. [And after describing certain sufferings relating to her body, the saint continues.] And even these are nothing by comparison with the agony of my soul, an oppression, a suffocation and an affliction so deeply felt, and accompanied by such hopeless and distressing misery, that I cannot too forcefully describe it. ..... The fact is I cannot find words to describe that interior fire and that despair, which is greater than the most grievous tortures and pains. .... and I repeat that that interior fire and despair are the worst of all."

A remarkable vision, as I think the reader would agree. And as with all visions, it is necessary to give a brief interpretation of the symbols described therein, for there is always the need for understanding and interpretation in a vision. As indeed is the same with much of Scripture.

The pictures of the 'long narrow passage - the ground full of water which looked like filthy, evil-smelling mud and the hollow space scooped out of a wall' describe the state of the soul that has led an evil life and dies in that condition. St. Teresa's comment 'that all this was pleasant by comparison to what I felt there' enforces this understanding. The reference to 'many wicked-looking reptiles' are to the constant spate of horrible thoughts that flood into the mind of the soul that finds itself in that unfortunate position. And St. Teresa's mention of the 'interior fire and despair', which she tells us are the worst of all, is a description of the utter feeling of hopelessness and despair with which such a soul is invaded. It sees most clearly its horrible state, and also the opportunities that it had while living in the body of how this state could have been avoided, or at least mitigated, and this realisation is one which torments the soul most of all. Most of us can recall times in our lives when we have said or done something that we have afterwards bitterly regretted, and how such thoughts, which recur over and over again, make us writhe mentally and often keep us awake at night. But this pales into insignificance in comparison with the 'hell-state' in which the soul described by St Teresa finds itself.

The reader may accept what has been written above, but will then say: "But this may not necessarily apply to a soul that has taken its own life in a fit of despair. Surely most souls cannot be as evil as the one described." No doubt this may be true, but it must be born in mind that a soul that takes its own life in a fit of despair cannot but go into a much worse state of despair, or out of the frying pan into the fire, as said above. Here, it may be noted that it is not God that sends a soul to hell, or into a state which closely resembles that of hell, but the soul itself, and this is my understanding of the words of our Lord in Matthew 5:25/26: "Be at agreement with thy adversary betimes, whilst thou art in the way with him: lest perhaps the adversary deliver thee to the judge, and the judge deliver thee to the officer, and thou be cast into prison. Amen I say to thee, thou shalt not go out from thence till thou repay the last farthing." Scholars have interpreted these words as being descriptive of a very severe state of purgatory.

Only absolute purity can experience the vision of God as He is in Himself, that is, in His Essence, as Scripture and the saints teach. So even though a soul that takes its own life is not cast into hell, it may find itself in a 'hell-state' from which only the mercy of God can rescue it. Now, since the mercy of God is boundless and unfathomable, as is His Nature, some will say that because a soul that takes his own life cannot have been in its right mind, it is certainly possible, even probable, that God, in His mercy, will forgive that soul. I would be the last one to argue against this, but I do not think that we should take such things for granted, for that would be to commit the sin of presumption, which is a serious one in its own right. Prevention is better than a cure.

Despair is not only contrary to Faith and Hope, but it destroys them. Faith and Hope are two of the three Theological Virtues (the other one being Charity or Love), and they are so called because they lead the soul directly to God, who resides in the deepest part of the soul. The saints have greatly extolled the virtue of Faith, and here it may be noted that we are not talking about a faith which many people refer to as blind, but Faith which, truly speaking, is a power that is developed by the soul, especially when the soul exercises itself in mortification and prayer. Faith includes Hope, since these two great virtues are inextricably intertwined.

So I say to those persons for whom this essay has been written, firmly establish and fortify your beachhead by calling on the holy name of our Lord Jesus Christ, as the title of this essay suggests, and allow the rays of the Son of God to dispel the mists of the negative thoughts in your minds. This will not be easy at first, but practice will make the mind and the soul more receptive. Then, instead of going to Beachy Head with thoughts of taking your life, you will go there to admire the beauty of God's Creation, which will banish away despair and replace it with Faith and Hope.

THE IMPACT OF EVENTS IN THE MIDDLE EAST ON WORLD HISTORY

If we cast our minds back through the history of the world, we can see that one major circumstance seems to stand out, which is the impact that events in the Middle East have had on world history. The foundation of this observation can be found in Scripture. But first, we can see a major event taking place in our own times. This is the mass migration of people from Syria, caused by the Civil War that is taking place there and the actions of the fanatical faction of Islam known as ISIS. This is causing upheaval not only in the Middle East, but also in Europe, and we have yet to see the end of it, what to speak of the events that will take place in the future as a result of it.

Now let us turn to Scripture. Over four thousand years ago, we have the revelation of God to Abraham; this revelation continued in the call of Moses and the great Jewish prophets, and the promise of the Messiah to come. After many vicissitudes, God finally established the Jewish people in their homeland in Palestine, as He had promised Moses. But the Jewish people later fell away from God; they disdained His commandments, worshipped idols and became very worldly indeed. In consequence, they were punished by God in the form of the two dispersions of the tribes of Israel and Judah that took place through the agency of the Assyrian and Babylonian empires. Here, we may note that the ancient kingdoms of Assyria and Babylonia are now part of the modern state of Iraq, a major country in the Middle East, and we know from our own times the turmoil that has taken place and is still taking place in that region. These were and are very turbulent times, to which we can perhaps relate today.

But today, we don't worship sticks and stones made by the hand of man; we have other, more sophisticated idols such as the Internet, television, and other electronic playthings. We all know where we stand in relation to them. This is not to say that we should not make use of these modern inventions, but how many of us use them as one would a useful tool instead of frittering much of our time away in useless pursuits? We forget what the great Italian saint, St. Alphonsus Liguori, the founder of the Redemptorist Religious Order, told us. He said that if we waste just one minute of our time on Earth, we can never recapture it. So, we are no better than the ancient people of the kingdoms of Israel and Judah. Can we then expect more preferential treatment from God than He gave to the Jewish people of those days? I don't think so.

The next major event in the lives of the Jewish people was their re-establishment in Palestine through the agency of King Cyrus and succeeding kings of Persia (present-day Iran). In those days, the Kingdom of Persia was very sympathetic to the Jews, as we can read in the books of Esdras, Nehemias and Esther in the Old Testament. It is interesting to contrast this with the enmity that present-day Iran bears to Israel. Again, these events took place in the Middle East and adjoining kingdoms.

The other major events that fulfilled prophecy were the rise of the Roman Empire, which embraced much of the known world at that time, including the land of the Jewish State in Palestine, and the coming of our Lord and Saviour Jesus Christ, one thousand plus years after the death of King David. But the Jewish rulers did not accept Him as the promised Messiah; they handed Him over to the Roman power to be crucified. This had to be, because without the sacrifice of Jesus Christ, there would have been no redemption and consequently, no forgiveness of our sins. Subsequently, the third and last dispersion of the Jewish people took place at the hands of the Roman Empire. Again, all of these events took place in the Middle East. Then we have the establishment of Christianity through the teachings of Jesus given through His instruments, the Apostles. Christianity has now spread all over the world, but let us not forget that it was first established in the Middle East even though the centre of Catholic Christianity later moved to Rome.

Here, we may also note that God still kept His promise to the Jewish people as we may read in the prophets, in that He finally re-established them in the State of Israel. This happened in 1948, once again, a major event that has taken place in the Middle East, and a very significant event indeed for the world.

To conclude, it is evident that events in the Middle East still take centre stage. The Western World, that is U.S.A., Canada, Europe and the UK are all caught up in these events in one way or another, and no doubt heartily wish that they would go away. But God will have the last word, which we have still to witness. And we can ask ourselves what this means. Are we in the 'last days' spoken of in Scripture, especially by Jesus Himself? Has the power of the Antichrist been released, as foretold in both the Old and New Testaments? Monsignor Eugene Kevane, Ph.D, a Catholic priest who wrote the book "The Deposit of Faith: What the Catholic Church Really Believes", seems to have thought so, and he quotes Pope St. Pius X and Cardinal John Henry Newman in support of this. We can all speculate, but there is little doubt in my mind that the grand denouement or last scenes of this epic world production will take place on the world stage of the Middle East. World events certainly seem to be coming to some sort of climax, and by this, we can understand the great apostasy from God that has taken place in our own day. How long will God continue to tolerate this situation? Does this mean that the Second Coming of our Lord, in whatever form that will take place, will also happen in the Middle East, more specifically, Jerusalem? We are certainly living in interesting times.

ON ADAM AND EVE

Theology tells us that the Holy Bible contains four meanings:

The Literal meaning
The Moral meaning
The Allegorical meaning
The Anagogical meaning

The first two meanings require no explanation. The allegorical meaning is that of spiritual truths, expressed in the outer garb of ordinary language and often couched in the form of stories we can all relate to. The parables of Our Lord are a good example of allegories, although they also partake of the anagogical element. The anagogical meaning belongs strictly to the hidden, mystical meaning contained in Scripture, and is the language of true mystics. By these I mean those great souls who have risen high into the Godhead and experienced God in His Essence, a state known as 'becoming God by participation', which is far beyond that of ecstasy, which is not lasting. Examples of such souls would be St. John of the Cross, St. Teresa of Avila, Johann Tauler, Richard of St. Victor, St. Bernard of Clairvaux, St. Dominic, St. Francis of Assisi, St. Francis de Sales, and St. Catherine of Sienna and many others, known and unknown, who lived between the 4th and 17th centuries, which I consider to be the allegorical, thousand year period referred to in chapter 20 of the Apocalypse. In this regard, I follow the views expressed by higher authority, and have written on this subject elsewhere.

The phrase 'becoming God by participation' is taken from Scripture, and appears in 2 Peter 1:4, where in speaking of God and Christ Jesus, the Apostle tells us: 'By whom he hath given us most great precious promises: that by these you may be made **partakers of the divine nature:** flying the corruption of that concupiscence which is in the world.' We are also told the same truth in Genesis 1:27, where it is said: 'And God created man to his own image; to the image of God he created him. Male and female, he created them.' We also read in Psalm 81:6, that: 'I have said: You are gods, and all of you the sons of the most High.' [Our Lord quoted this verse in John 10:34]

Christ's Sermon on the Mount in chapters 5 to 7 in the Gospel of St. Matthew contains a wealth of material that is moral, allegorical and anagogical in nature. Good examples of allegory are the parables of the sower, the cockle among the wheat, likening the kingdom of heaven to a mustard seed, and the pearl of great price, all of which can be found in Matthew 13. But those parables too can be given an anagogical meaning. Even Our Lord's disciples did not understand the parable of the cockle among the wheat, and asked Him to explain it to them (Matthew 13:36/43).

Another example of the anagogical meaning can be found in chapter 12 of 2 Corinthians, wherein St. Paul tells us: 'I know a man in Christ: above fourteen years ago (whether in the body, I know not, or out of the body, I know not; God knoweth), such a one caught up to the third heaven....... That he was caught up into paradise and heard secret words which it is not granted to man to utter.' St. Paul did not explain further on this, but his experience was a purely a mystical one, and no doubt, extremely difficult to put into words.

The Books of the Prophets in the Old Testament contain all four meanings noted above. The Psalms, as well as being songs of praise and worship of God, contain much that is both allegorical and anagogical in meaning, as well as containing moral teachings. The Song of Songs (or the Canticle of the Canticles as it is also known) is, I would say, almost entirely anagogical in its meaning, as is the Apocalypse in the New Testament.

God speaks to us throughout Scripture, and His language is extremely difficult to comprehend for ordinary mortals. This we know from Isaias 55: 8/9, wherein God tells us through the Prophet: 'For my thoughts are not your thoughts, nor your ways my ways, saith the Lord. For as the heavens are exalted above the earth, so are my ways exalted above your ways, and my thoughts above your thoughts.' Similarly, in the Book of Wisdom 9:13, we find: 'For who among men is he that can know the counsel of God? Or who can think what the will of God is?'

All this is not to say that the anagogical part of Scripture must remain a closed book to mortals, for God has in the past revealed His secrets to His chosen friends, and can do so in the present and the future, provided we are willing to pay the price of the sacrifice of our wills to the Will of God by living a life that is founded on the virtues, the practice of mortification, and prayer, especially the practice of contemplative prayer, wherein souls can experience the dark night of the soul, so well described by St. John of the Cross.

We come now to the story of Adam and Eve, as related in the Book of Genesis in the Old Testament. Genesis contains all four meanings of Scripture noted above, especially the anagogical, but how are we to understand the story of Adam and Eve? There seems to be little doubt that Adam and Eve are representative of the image of mankind, both male and female. Here, we may note that mystics understand that the mysterious Being we call God, although He is pure Spirit, in a manner we cannot comprehend, manifests within Himself both masculine and feminine principles. So, in creating man in His image (Genesis 1:26/27), we are told that 'male and female he created them' (Genesis 1:27), 'male' being the image of the masculine principle contained in God, and 'female' being the image of the feminine principle.

It can also be said that the masculine principle of God manifests itself in the form of the Justice of God, and the feminine principle in the form of the Mercy of God. In ancient times, the Jewish people were subject to the Justice of God in the form of severe punishments and the dispersions of Israel and Judah throughout the world, while His Mercy is very evident in the birth of the Virgin Mary and the Incarnation of His Son, our Lord Jesus Christ. And because the world (especially the Christian world) has in large part spurned the incomprehensible sacrifice of Christ in which He took the sins of humanity, past present, and future, on His human soul, I think that the world is in for a healthy dose of the masculine principle of Justice. One can get some idea of the form that this will take by reading chapter 24 of the Gospel of St. Matthew, which describes the punishment that is in store in highly symbolic terms.

For the reasons given above, when members of the same sex lie together, Scripture uses the strongest language in condemning such an act, because it is an affront of the greatest magnitude to the Nature of God. The relevant verses in Scripture follow:

Leviticus 18:22: Thou shalt not lie with mankind as with womankind: because it is an abomination.

Leviticus 20:13: If any one lie with a man as with a woman, both have committed an abomination: let them be put to death. Their blood be upon them.

Deuteronomy 22:5: A woman shall not be clothed with man's apparel: neither shall a man use woman's apparel. For he that doeth these things is abominable before God.

3 Kings 14:24: There were also the effeminate in the land: and they did according to all the abominations of the people whom the Lord had destroyed before the face of the children of Israel.

Romans 1:26/27: For this cause, God delivered them up to shameful affections. For their women have changed the natural use into that use which is against nature. And, in like manner, the men also, leaving the natural use of the woman, have burned in their lusts, one towards another: men with men, working that which is filthy and receiving in themselves the recompense which was due to their error.

To excuse such behaviour on the grounds that certain persons who are born in one sex or the other possess feelings or emotions of the opposite sex and say "I'm born that way" cannot, in my opinion, be used to justify such behaviour, no more than can a member of the male sex justify his actions in sexually abusing a woman by pleading that he was subject to an overpowering sexual desire at the time. We should be very cautious when we try to justify our lifestyle by claiming "I am made that way", since what we first cultivate by habit and desire becomes nature, and we then convince ourselves that we were born that way.

I am not denying that there are genuine cases where a person born as a man or a woman feels that he or she were born in the wrong sex, and that there are even those rare cases where a person's sex is physically part one and part the other. In either case, the important thing to remember is that the soul is the true person, not the physical body in which it dwells. Although it may be asking a great deal of such persons, I suggest that the most fruitful act they can do is to offer up their suffering as a sacrifice to God. What they should not do is to satisfy their sensual desires in unnatural ways that are offensive to God. And the same thing applies to those who are normal and seek to satisfy their sensual nature without let or hindrance. And it is no different in the state of lawful marriage. The saints have taught that although one duty of marriage may be to beget children, an even more important one is that married couples should help one another to draw closer to God. And there are numerous opportunities for that given the often stressful situations that can arise in the married state once the early glamour of the relationship has worn off. As I mentioned in another essay, it is not acceptable to God if we live a worldly life, and then in our middle age, when we have exhausted most of our passions and energies, to say: 'Now, God, we will give you some time to You.' Any reasonable person who is offered a gift of something second or third hand would not be pleased with it; similarly, it is no gift to God to offer Him a worn-out shell. And if we consider the matter, if we offer God our best in our youth, are we not offering Him something which we first received from Him as a free gift!

Scripture is very clear on the relationship that should exist between a man and a woman, for in Genesis 2:24, we are told: 'Wherefore a man shall leave father and mother, and shall cleave to his wife: and they shall be two in one flesh.' To my understanding, this verse has both a literal meaning and an anagogical or mystical meaning. The literal meaning tells us about the close relationship that should exist between man and wife, and the anagogical or mystical meaning speaks of the uniting of the male and female principles into one, of becoming God by participation, thus restoring fallen man to the image of God in which he was originally created.

It is also worth noting that Genesis 2:21/23 is the Scriptural authority for the marriage vows, in which the wife-to-be promises to love, honour and obey the husband-to-be. This is symbolised in Genesis 2:21/23 in the following words:

> "Then the Lord God cast a deep sleep upon Adam: and when he was fast asleep, he took one of his ribs, and filled up flesh for it. And the Lord God built the rib which he took from Adam into a woman: and brought her to Adam. And Adam said: This now is bone of my bones, and flesh of my flesh; she shall be called woman, because she was taken out of man."

Very few of us were born saints. Scripture testifies to this, for in Genesis 8:21, we read: '...... for the imagination and thought of man's heart are prone to evil from his youth......' Nevertheless, given that we were created in the image of God and can become God by participation as set out above, it is incumbent upon us to make the best use of the time at our disposal, for as the Church teaches, after death, we cannot merit. It is our task to sublimate our human nature as best we can, for we were put on earth for no other purpose. The situations, challenges and difficulties we all experience are but a means to this end.

To return to the main purpose of this essay, I would like to make the following additional observations on what has been said above on the mystery of the symbolism of Adam and Eve, and how we can understand it in terms of the times in which we live.

We are told in Genesis 2:7 that God 'formed man of the slime of the earth, and breathed into his face the breath of life; and man became a living soul'. So although God created man in His image (a figure for the higher part of man's soul), man was also formed of the slime of the earth (a figure for the physical body and the lower part of his soul, in which reside the imagination, the passions and desires). It is important to bear this in mind for the conclusions that are drawn from Adam's fall and the part that Eve played in this.

The name 'Adam' first appears in the second chapter of Genesis (verses 19/23, 25), and it is in this chapter that he is given a helpmate, for God said that 'It is not good for man to be alone; let us make him a help like unto himself' (verse 18). But it is not until Genesis 3:20 that 'Adam called the name of his wife Eve: because she was the mother of all the living'. We are also told in Genesis 5:1/2 that: 'In the day that God created man, he made him to the likeness of God. He created them male and female; and blessed them; and called them their name Adam, in the day when they were created'. So from all this, we can conclude that the figure of Adam is very mysterious and from the point of view of understanding its meaning, is highly anagogical in nature.

Now we come to the Fall of man. The great mystic saints tell us that in the higher part of the soul reside the three spiritual faculties of the Understanding, the Will and the Memory. They are not in themselves the image of God within us, but form part of that image. These three faculties are therefore in man, as well as the lower faculties referred to above. This lower part of man is well described in verse 16 of chapter 2 of the First Epistle of St. John, wherein he tells us: 'For all that is in the world is the concupiscence of the flesh and the concupiscence of the eyes and the pride of life, which is not of the Father but is of the world.' So, when God told Adam: 'But of the tree of knowledge of good and evil, thou shalt not eat. For in what day soever thou shalt eat of it, thou shalt die the death' (Genesis 2:17), the stage was set for the Fall of Man, for Eve, who represents the feminine principle, also represents 'desire', or a combination of the 'concupiscence of the flesh and of the eyes and the pride of life'.

But Adam listened to his wife Eve (who represents desire), and being tempted by the serpent (who represents Satan), the result was that both ate of the fruit of the tree of good and evil (Genesis 3:6), and 'the eyes of them both were opened: and they perceived themselves to be naked....' (Genesis 3:7). The rest of the story is contained in Genesis 3, and the results we know, for we only have to look at the state of humanity today, which for the most part is a combination of the 'concupiscence of the flesh and of the eyes and the pride of life'.

What was God's solution to the problem? There was only one solution; God Himself had to fix it, and He did this when He created the Blessed Virgin Mary, the Virgin of all virgins, who became the chosen vessel through whom Jesus Christ, the Saviour of mankind, and the Second Person of the Trinity, took flesh and became man for our salvation. But given my above comments on the rejection by the world of God's plan for our salvation, the future of mankind bodes ill.

The first four chapters of Genesis (and also succeeding chapters) are a perfect example of the anagogical meaning of Scripture. Although one would need to be enlightened by God Himself in order to gain an understanding of their full import, this does not prevent one from having some understanding of their meaning, provided that one can support this by a reasonable interpretation of Scripture.

ON ADVENT AND LENT

ADVENT

According to the Catechism of the Catholic Church, the time of Advent "makes present this ancient expectancy of the Messiah, for by sharing in the long preparation for the Saviour's first coming, the faithful renew their ardent desire for His second coming......"

Over the centuries, the emphasis in preparing for Advent has been on outer things. We decorate our homes and Christmas trees with lights, and spend much energy and money shopping for gifts and Christmas cards. Christmas used to be a time of magic for children, but no more. It is unnecessary to belabour the point that the time of Advent has degenerated into a worldly celebration. Everywhere, we find a spiritual lethargy.

To put us into the right frame of mind in considering the true meaning of Advent, let us recall that the Christ Child was born in a stable, "because there was no room for them in the inn". The Christ Child entered the world in material poverty, but He brought with Him spiritual riches for our souls that we have yet to comprehend. Even the gifts He was given by the Three Wise Men do not signify worldly riches. Gold signified His spiritual kingship; myrrh the bitterness He suffered from the ingratitude of those He came to save; frankincense the prayers He offered up to His Father for humanity, and which culminated in the ultimate prayer of His sacrifice on the Cross.

So Advent truly means and requires that we live the interior life. It means that we must take up our cross and deny ourselves. The second coming is not an event that is in our hands to hasten. But it is in our hands to bring about the Advent of Christ in our own lives, and by this, we mean the dawning of God in our hearts. When we talk about the dawning of God in our hearts, we are not talking about experiencing visions or apparitions, but the touch of the Essence of God Himself in the deepest part of our souls. This has been described by the great mystics of Catholicism such as St. John of the Cross, St. Teresa of Avila, Johann Tauler and many others, not all of them of the Catholic tradition. What we are trying to say here, is that a true experience of God may be had in our lifetime by each one of us if we are willing to enter the spiritual battle, for as Christ Himself said in Matthew 6:24:

> "No man can serve two masters. For either he will hate the one, and love the other: or he will sustain the one and despise the other. You cannot serve God and mammon."

This preparation of Advent is not a matter of four weeks in order to prepare ourselves for the celebration of the birth of Christ on Christmas Day; it is a preparation of a lifetime; it is to practise the abstinence of the Lenten time our whole life long.

People will no doubt hold up their hands in horror at being told that one must practise abstinence as a way of life in order to prepare for the Advent of Christ in our lives. But this is no new thing. The saints did it, and went to extremes of mortification, both in exterior and interior disciplines. For those of us who live in the world, God does not ask this of us. But one of His great saints, St. Francis de Sales, recommended the middle way of treading this path. He tells us that while we are not expected to imitate the saints in all their rigour, we can follow them closely, or at the very least, at a distance. This is not as difficult as it may seem, but it does require that we live in this world as non-permanent residents. In enjoying the good things of life, we must practise moderation in all things, especially in the partaking of food. More will be said about this when we speak of the requirements of Lent.

We won't lose the fruit of our efforts even if we do not experience the ineffable touch of God in our souls as a result of our efforts to live a more disciplined life, for we carry the merit with us when we pass from this life for, as the Church teaches, we can only merit in this life, not after death.

LENT

In the Season of Lent, three spiritual disciplines are stressed. These are: Penance, Fasting, and Almsgiving. On these three principles, the Catechism tells us that:

"The interior penance of the Christian can be expressed in many and various ways. Scripture and the Fathers (of the Church) insist above all on three forms, fasting, prayer and almsgiving, which expresses conversion in relation to oneself, to God and to others." [1434]. Also,

"The way of perfection passes by the way of the Cross. There is no holiness without renunciation and spiritual battle. Spiritual progress entails the ascesis (practice of self-discipline) and mortification that gradually lead to living in the peace and joy of the Beatitudes." [2015]

It is clear that since there is no holiness without renunciation and spiritual battle, it is fruitless to restrict the efforts we must make in this direction to the Seasons of Advent and Lent. As we have already said, it is a preparation of a lifetime. When fasting is recommended to us, this is not restricted to abstaining from food completely for a certain period, although this is certainly one meaning of the word. It is far better to follow the principle of 'we eat to live, not live to eat.' A saint once said that we should always leave the table feeling as though we could eat more. The discipline of the palate is particularly difficult for most people, because the temptation to overeat, and also to eat a variety of the most tastiest of foods, is always before us. But unless we control the palate, which comes under the capital sin of gluttony, it will not be possible to master the other and more difficult capital sins of anger, lust, and sloth. And unless we begin to achieve a degree of mastery over the exterior aspects of these sins, in which we give them outer expression, it is simply not possible to begin to master their far more important and difficult interior aspects, which we need in order to develop virtues such as patience, fortitude, meekness and inner purity. If we think that we can develop these interior virtues without first obtaining mastery over the exterior ones, we simply delude ourselves.

A very useful thing to know in this spiritual battle between the higher man and the lower man is that a saint once said that at least 80% of worldly impressions enter through the eyes. We can demonstrate this in Scripture, for in his first Epistle, St. John tells us that:

"For all that is in the world, is the concupiscence of the flesh, and the concupiscence of the eyes, and the pride of life, which is not of the Father, but is of the world."

Concupiscence is simply another name for desire, and most of the ills that affect us in the concupiscence of the flesh, whether of gluttony or lust, enter through the eyes. For this reason, our Lord tells us in Matthew 5:29:

"And if thy right eye scandalize thee, pluck it out and cast it from thee. For it is expedient for thee that one of thy members should perish, rather than that thy whole body be cast into hell."

Here, our Lord is telling us that we need to govern the sense of sight in order to preserve the integrity of our soul. He emphasizes this, when He tells us in Matthew 6:22/23:

"The light of thy body is thy eye. If thy eye be single, thy whole body shall be lightsome. But if thy eye be evil thy whole body shall be darksome. If then the light that is in thee be darkness: the darkness itself how great shall it be!"

This verse also refers to prayer, and as further explained below, to restraining the wandering of the mind, which is a very common problem, especially in the practice of contemplative prayer, which unlike vocal or oral prayer, is when we strive to put our full attention on God. The great spiritual classic, the Ascent of Mount Carmel, by St. John of the Cross, explains this difficulty in great detail.

The Catechism also puts an emphasis on prayer during Lent. But since we cannot walk the road to true holiness unless we practice mortification throughout our lives, so must we also practise a life of prayer, or spiritual almsgiving, which is far more valuable than the giving of our substance in almsgiving as it is generally understood. We can even say that prayer is a spiritual almsgiving to God, since when we pray, we are giving time to God. There is no more valuable gift that we can give to God than prayer, because we are doing that which our human nature finds very difficult, since people usually complain that they find prayer very tedious, and get no pleasure from it. But it is in the very effort we make to pray that is constituted the gift, and that gift becomes more valuable the more we persevere in it.

Needless to say, God will not be outdone in generosity, for as our Lord tells us in Matthew 6:19/21:

"Lay not up to yourselves treasures on earth: where the rust, and moth consume, and where thieves break through and steal. But lay up to yourselves treasures in heaven: where neither the rust nor moth doth consume, and where thieves do not break through, nor steal. For where thy treasure is, there is thy heart also."

That treasure is prayer, and when it is combined with dryness, which often happens when practising the prayer of recollection, the value of what we offer to God is infinitely enhanced. The author of The Spiritual Combat, a book that was a favourite with St. Francis de Sales, tells us:

"For the prayers and spiritual exercises of the soul, deprived of all satisfaction in what she does, is the delight of the Almighty, according to St. Gregory. Particularly is such a soul pleasing to God if, notwithstanding its insensibility and apathy, it persists with courage. For the patience of such a soul is a prayer in itself, prevailing more with God than any prayers said with great emotional fervour......"

Whether we practice vocal prayer, mental prayer, or contemplative prayer (the earlier stage of which is known as the prayer of recollection), we should strive to do so with full attention. The tendency of the mind to wander is greatest in contemplative prayer, for such is the distaste of the mind for doing something that it does not enjoy, that it easily wanders off. That is why St Teresa of Avila advised that true vocal prayer cannot be divorced from mental prayer, in which we reflect on one of the mysteries of the Rosary, or on a passage from Scripture, or simply speak to God in our hearts. In this regard, Johann Tauler, a great mystic soul of the 14th century, tells us that:

"True prayer is not a lot of babbling with the lips, so many psalms and so many vigils, clattering your beads and letting your heart wander up and down. Prayer which is prayed in the spirit is infinitely superior to all external prayer. Our Father wants us to pray to Him in this way, and all other kinds of prayer are only to help us towards such prayers. ...." And: "To praise God in silence is beyond all comparison the highest of these three forms of praise."

The saints have described praising God in silence as the lifting up of the heart and mind to God. Tauler describes this as loving Him ardently, and wanting Him in the depths of our souls, with all our intellect and all our reason. People may raise the objection that this is precisely what they cannot do and that they cannot manufacture such feelings and desires. But this is to misunderstand what Tauler is saying, for when we pray without receiving any consolations, and if we persevere in this, we are truly wanting Him in the depths of our souls, with all our intellect and all our reason.

We can do no better in speaking on prayer than to quote our Lord, where in Matthew 6:6/8, He advises us:

> "But when thou shalt pray, enter into thy chamber, and having shut the door, pray to thy Father in secret: and thy Father who seeth in secret will repay thee. And when you are praying, speak not much, as the heathens. For they think that in their much speaking, they may be heard. Be not you therefore like to them; for your Father knoweth what is needful for you, before you ask him."

The chamber referred to by our Lord is our soul and shutting the door refers to closing down the outer senses.

And in Luke 17: 20/21:

> "And being asked by the Pharisees when the Kingdom of God should come, he answered them and said: The kingdom of God cometh not with observation: Neither shall they say: Behold here, or behold there. For lo, the kingdom of God is within you."

Finally, the question arises as to how long we should spend in prayer. The only answer to this question is the longer the better. However, to be practical, those who are beginners should strive to put in half an hour first thing in the morning and half an hour before retiring for the night. Perhaps they will have to build up to this; however, the secret is to persevere, for perseverance builds up a desire and hunger for the time we spend alone with God. The rest we must leave to Him.

ON THE RESURRECTION

In his essay, Fern-seed and Elephants, in the book of the same name, C.S. Lewis took certain theologians of the 'modern school' to task, chastising them for their pretended omniscience and their pretense to know more, as a result of so-called modern scholarship, than did the disciples of Christ, and those who succeeded them in the early years of Christianity. C.S. Lewis likened such theologians to persons who claimed to see fern seed but couldn't spot an elephant ten yards away in broad daylight.

It seems that we now have a resurgence of this spurious 'enlightened thinking', as exemplified by certain priests and religious who are questioning the resurrection of Jesus Christ. At this point, it is well to note that much modern scholarship appears to rest, in part, upon claims that certain Scriptures were not necessarily written by the Apostles, but were written at a later date by others. There are probably so many variations on this theme that one would need to be a 'scholar' oneself in order to challenge many of these bogus assertions, which is something to be wondered at, since they constitute a direct challenge to the spirituality and scholarship of St. Jerome, who gave us the Vulgate, or Latin, version of the Bible, from which the Douay-Rheims version of the Bible was translated. Since St. Jerome lived during the fourth century A.D, it is clear that he was much closer to the lives and times of the Apostles and their immediate successors than modern scholars, and as already mentioned, he was himself a great scholar.

Both the Old and New Testaments are revealed Scripture. Either the Scriptures have a Divine Author as their foundation and inspiration, or they do not. That certain incidents related in the Synoptic Gospels differ cannot be denied. However, to my mind, this is a proof of their genuineness, in that these differences in detail go to prove the authenticity of the teachings and events described. It would be amazing indeed if the writers of the three Synoptic Gospels agreed in every small particular. If this had been so, to my mind, this in itself would have cast suspicion as to the truthfulness of the events related. As to the Gospel of St. John, we should bear in mind that St. John lived to a great age, and it is reasonable to conclude that he would have been intimately familiar with what had already been written by Matthew, Mark, and Luke, and that for completeness, he wrote about those events that he himself had witnessed, but which were omitted by the other Apostles of our Lord. This would account for the great difference between the Gospel of St. John and the three Synoptic Gospels. Some scholars have even queried if the Book of the Apocalypse (or Book of Revelation as is also known), was written by St. John, since it is so different from his Gospel. But one does not have to be a scholar to give a definitive answer to that, since a reading of both reveals that the former is essentially prophetic, containing mysteries and secrets of God which the apostle would have received in a state of spiritual consciousness, and even common sense should tell us that such subject matter would be quite different from the latter, which is a narration of the teachings and events in the life our Lord that took place during the lifetime of St. John. But even so, the opening verses of the Gospel of St. John, which are among the most powerful and momentous statements in Scripture, are surely a foretaste of the enigmatic writings of the Apocalypse that came later.

After this digression, and to return to the main subject of this essay, one could be pardoned if he should ask the question as to whether those who presume to plumb the depths of the mysteries and secrets of God, including the writer of this essay, have mastered just one passion, or if they have conquered their predominant sin (i.e. the one in which they offend God the most)? Or whether they have practised such self-denial as would please God, and which would go some way to make them receptive to His promptings through the Holy Spirit? Christ Himself said in Matthew 16:24 that: 'If any man will come after me, let him deny himself, and take up his cross, and follow me.' For it should be borne in mind that in order to become a friend of God and to merit the grace to have an understanding of His mysteries, it is necessary to conform every aspect of our lives to His Nature. This is what St. John of the Cross and others meant when they said that a soul can become God by participation. This is not achieved by study or scholarship or any refinement of the intellect of man. In order for the intellect of man to know divine truths, it must be enlightened by rays of God's intellect, and in the words of St. John of the Cross as taken from Book III, Chapter V of the Ascent of Mount Carmel (hereinafter referred to as the "Ascent"):

'….. For, in order to approach God, the soul must proceed by not comprehending rather than by comprehending; it must exchange the mutable and comprehensible for the immutable and incomprehensible.'

The lives of the Saints have proved this principle, and further, to quote from Book II, Chapter VII of the Ascent, where St. John of the Cross is talking about the living death of the Cross, both as to sense and as to spirit - that is, both outwardly and inwardly, he says:

'I will not pursue this subject farther, although I have no desire to finish speaking of it, for I see that Christ is known very little by those who consider themselves His friends: we see them seeking in Him their own pleasures and consolations because of their great love for themselves, but not loving His bitter trials and His death because of their great love for Him. I am speaking now of those who consider themselves His friends; for such as live far away, withdrawn from Him, men of great learning and influence, and all others who live yonder, with the world, and are eager about their ambitions and their prelacies, may be said not to know Christ; and their end, however good, will be very bitter. Of such I make no mention in these lines; but mention will be made of them on the Day of Judgment, for to them it was fitting to speak first this word of God, as to those whom

God set up as a target for it, by reason of their learning and their high position.'

These are strong words, coming as they do from one of the greatest mystical doctors and theologians given by God to the Catholic Church. Those about whom St. John of the Cross is speaking are the 'wolves in sheep's clothing' spoken of in Matthew 7:15.

Therefore, to question the Resurrection of Christ is to question the Passion itself; it is to question Christ's own words, when in the Gospel of St. John 2:19:

'Jesus answered and said unto them, destroy this temple, and in three days I will raise it up'

It is to deny the witness of St. Paul, when in 1 Corinthians 15:12/17, he said:

'Now if Christ be preached, that he rose again from the dead, how do some among you say that there is no resurrection of the dead? But if there be no resurrection of the dead, then is Christ not risen again. And if Christ be not risen again, then is our preaching vain, and your faith is also vain. Yea, and we are found false witnesses of God; because we have given testimony against God, that he raised up Christ; whom he hath not raised up, if the dead rise not again. For if the dead rise not again, neither is Christ risen again, and if Christ be not risen again, your faith is vain; for you are yet in your sins.'

It is to deny the witness of the five hundred or so who saw Christ after He was crucified and died. It is to deny the witness of the two men who were on their way to Emmaus when Christ met with them [Luke 24]. Finally, it is to deny the raising of Lazarus from the dead, as well as the other miracles, when Jesus raised the daughter of Jairus from the dead [Matthew

9 and Luke 8], and raised the widow's son from the dead [Luke 7]. Those priests and religious who deny the Resurrection of our Lord are also a type of 'wolves in sheep's clothing', who are known by their fruits.

In the quote from 1 Corinthians, St. Paul was indirectly referring to the belief in the resurrection of the dead by the Pharisees, and the lack of belief on the part of the Sadducees. This does not imply that the Jews of that time, who believed in the resurrection, were speaking about the resurrection of the body made of flesh, blood and bones, i.e. the physical body. That the physical body of Jesus was resurrected is incontrovertible, and it is also incontrovertible that Christ had both a human nature and a divine nature. However, unlike us, Jesus was fully the master of the lower part of the soul, which is part of our human nature. Yes, He felt and suffered pain, and the torture of the Passion, but what we cannot say is that like ourselves, Jesus was also subject to the frailties of human nature. I sometimes wonder whether some writers consider Jesus to be either a glorified saint or a deficient god.

That the body of Jesus was superior to the laws of nature after His resurrection can be understood from the incident during which he broke bread for the two men whom he met on the way to Emmaus, and then vanished from their sight, and also the incident of His appearance to the disciples in the Upper Room. Although Jesus did not often manifest these powers over His body before He was crucified, there are one or two hints that He occasionally used them. For example, in John 6 and Matthew 14, the disciples saw Jesus walking on water, clearly a sign that He had full mastery of His body. Also, as described in John 7, when Jesus told the Jews that '....I am not come of myself, but he that sent me is true, whom you know not. I know him, because I am from him, and he hath sent me'...., they sought to apprehend him: and no man laid hands on him, because his hour was not yet come, And in John 8, when Jesus told the Jews in the temple that: '.... Before Abraham was made, I am......' [declaring Himself to be God] they took up stones therefore to cast at

Him. But Jesus hid himself, and went out of the temple.' By "hid himself", I understand that He vanished from their sight, just as He did after breaking bread for the two men whom He met on the way to Emmaus. A similar incident is narrated in John 10.

To return to what St. Paul said in 1 Corinthians 15: '…. For if the dead rise not again, neither is Christ risen again; and if Christ be not risen again, your faith is in vain; for you are yet in your sins.', he was explaining that the Resurrection of Christ was the fruit, the Scriptural proof of the great redemptive act of the Passion. To quote again from the Ascent, Book II, Chapter VII:

'…… it is certain that, at the moment of His death, He was likewise annihilated in His soul, and was deprived of any relief and consolation, since His Father left Him in the most interior aridity, according to the lower part of His nature. Wherefore He had perforce to cry out, saying: "My God! My God! Why hast Thou forsaken Me?" This was the greatest desolation, with respect to sense, that He had suffered in His life. And thus He wrought herein the greatest work that He had ever wrought, whether in miracles or in mighty works, during the whole of His life, either upon earth or in Heaven, which was the reconciliation and union of mankind, through grace, with God…..'

These words tell us that in some marvellous and mysterious fashion, God the Son, who in the momentous words of St. John, was the Word made flesh who dwelt among us, became for a brief moment of time, separated from God the Father. In this regard to understand Jesus' cry of abandonment on the Cross: "My God, My God, why hast Thou forsaken Me", one must link these words with his words in the Garden of Gethsemani, when He asked the Father to remove the chalice from Him. This was the chalice of the filth of sin of humanity, past, present, and future, that Jesus Christ took upon His human soul. This chalice necessarily included mortal sin, and as the Church teaches, mortal sin results in the loss of Sanctifying Grace, that is to say, man cuts himself off from God. And because the human soul of Jesus Christ absorbed this chalice of the filth of sin of humanity for a period of time unknown to us, be it a fleeting moment or longer, God the Son surrendered His Divinity on the Cross. It was this incomprehensible sacrifice that was the true sacrifice by which God the Son accomplished the Redemption of humanity. But it is to be noted that this was done, as St. John of the Cross explained in his work 'Ascent of Mount Carmel', Book II, Chapter VII, according to the lower part of His nature…. with respect to sense. That is to say, that this sacrifice by the Son of God of His Godhood could not have been done any other way than by His Incarnation, that is, by assuming human nature by being born as we are born, and by dying as we must die. And this is why the teaching of the Church that Christ had both a Divine Nature and a human nature is so profound, and goes to the very heart of the reason why God became man so that He could perform His great sacrificial act and rise again from the dead. In Volume Two, chapter XXXVIII of his monumental work, The Three Ages of The Interior Life, Fr. Reginald Garrigou-Lagrange describes this to perfection, when he wrote: "Christ's victory over sin and the devil on Good Friday is far greater than the victory He won over death by His Resurrection. The resurrection of His body is only a sign of the power He has to restore life to souls, to forgive them their sins."

Therefore, the Resurrection of Christ was the culminating act of His Passion, its proof, and also the fulfilment of Scripture. But it also has a most secret and profound meaning, and this relates to the resurrection of humanity in general, and in this lies the main reason why I think that people go astray in their understanding of the Resurrection of Christ as it relates to our resurrection. Pertinent to the subject, in Romans 6:4/5, St. Paul said:

'For we are buried together with him by baptism into death: that as Christ is risen from the dead by the glory of the Father, so we also may walk in newness of life. For if we have been planted together in the likeness of his death, we shall be also in the likeness of his resurrection.'

It is my understanding of the word "likeness" that I now wish to try to explain. I will commence by saying that the resurrection of the body as it applies to humanity, and which was accomplished and paid for by the sacrifice of Jesus Christ on the Cross, does not mean the resurrection of this body of flesh, blood and bone in which we now dwell, but the resurrection or restoration of what I call our inner body, on which more will be said below. In this regard, perhaps one of the most misunderstood parts of Scripture is that of Ezechiel 37, wherein is described the vision of the resurrection of the dry bones. Ezechiel was commanded by God to prophesy upon these bones, and upon doing so sinews and flesh came upon them and skin covered them, but there was no breath (i.e. soul) in them. Then Ezechiel was commanded to prophesy unto the wind, and breath came into them, and they lived. Ezechiel was then told by God that the bones represented the whole house of Israel, and the clothing of the bones in sinews and flesh and the breathing of life into them represented the restoration of Israel and Judah as one nation [Ezechiel 37:16/17]. That this event has already taken place, in that the State of Israel was re-established in Palestine in 1948, is a matter of history.

In interpreting Ezechiel's vision, we can also understand the restoration of the bones with sinews, flesh, but especially the breathing of life into them, as the redemption of humanity by the sacrifice of Jesus Christ. Another meaning of "resurrect" is to "restore", or in terms of Christ's redemptive act, the restoration of the soul to its pristine beauty as God originally created it. But if the Passion and death of our Lord and His subsequent Resurrection does not pertain to the resurrection of our flesh and blood bodies, then what does it mean? I think the answer lies in what St. Paul meant when he said: 'For if we have been planted together in the likeness of his death, we shall be also in the likeness of his resurrection'. [The last part of this essay attempts to describe how we can be led astray if we take the words and accompanying visions described in Scripture in a literal manner; this also applies to words (known as locutions) and the visions experienced by persons outside of Scripture in the past and present. We shall offer some brief comments on this topic, and in so doing, will have recourse to the teachings of St. John of the Cross, taken from the Ascent. Examples from Scripture will also be given.]

I have mentioned above my belief that we possess an inner body in addition to this physical body of flesh and blood, and a little further on, I shall refer to certain incidents from the life of Padre Pio and St. Martin de Porres to support this belief. But to digress a moment, I wish first to describe the mystical tradition of Judaism as contained in a book known as the Zohar, which means the Book of Splendour. I will then attempt to make a comparison of these teachings with the superior or higher part of the soul described in Catholic mysticism. Among the mystical teachings in the Zohar, there is a reference to the threefold make-up of man's soul, which is composed of nephesh (the vital or animal soul), ruah (spirit), and neshamah (innermost soul, super-soul). These three are comprehended one within the other, but each has its separate abode. Although an exact comparison cannot be made, I understand that 'nephesh' is equivalent or similar to the passions and emotions of the lower part of the soul described in the Catholic tradition; 'ruah' is equivalent or similar to the three faculties of the soul, being made up of the understanding, memory and will, that is also described in the Catholic tradition, while 'neshamah' is equivalent or similar to the image of God within us. The question may now be asked: where does this superior or higher part of the soul reside in the human body? The answer from the Catholic tradition is that it resides in the head, and I give the following four references to support this:

i)   In her book, the Interior Castle, St. Teresa of Avila tells us that: '.....

My head sounds just as if it were full of brimming rivers, and then as if all the water in those rivers came suddenly rushing downward; and a host of little birds seem to be whistling, not in the ears, but in the upper part of the head, where the higher part of the soul is said to be; I have held this view for a long time, for the spirit seems to move upward with great velocity... But if the higher part of the soul is in the upper part of the head, how is it that it experiences no disturbance? That I do not know, but I do know that what I say is true......'

ii) In Book III, Chapter II of the Ascent, in the course of discussing the purification of the natural apprehensions of the memory (one of the three faculties of the soul) St. John of the Cross tells us that: 'Now there sometimes comes to pass here a notable thing; for occasionally, when God brings about these touches of union in the memory, the brain (where memory has its seat) is so perceptibly upset that it seems as if it becomes quite inert, and its judgment and sense are lost.....'

iii) In an extract from the Revelations of St Gertrude, she relates that: 'On another occasion, when I was about to communicate at Mass, being filled abundantly with Thy Spirit, and seeking within myself what I could do in return for so great a favour, Thou didst propose to me, as a Master full of wisdom, these words of the Apostle: "I wish myself to be as an anathema for my brethren" (Rom. ix.). And although Thou hadst taught me before that the soul had its abode in the heart, Thou didst make me know also that it resides in the brain; and this truth, of which I had been ignorant until then, was confirmed to me afterwards by a testimony of Scripture.....'

iv) In Volume I of The Three Ages of The Interior Life, Fr. Garrigou-Lagrange tells us that: '...... far from being essentially extraordinary, the mystical life alone, which is characterized by the reality of the quasi-experimental knowledge of God present in us, is completely normal. Only the saints, all of whom live this sort of life, are fully in order. Before experiencing this intimate union with God present in us, we are somewhat like souls still half asleep, souls not yet spiritually awakened...... The Holy Ghost is the soul of the mystical body, of which Christ is the head. As in our body the soul is entirely in the whole body and entirely in each part, and exercises its superior functions in the head, so the Holy Ghost is entirely in all the mystical body, entirely in each soul, and exercises His highest functions in the holy soul of the Savior, and through it on us......'

Since the superior or higher part of the soul survives death, it is only natural to ask ourselves the question: but what form does it take? The simple answer is that it takes the human form, and I think that common sense would tell us that it can take no other. After the death of the body, the superior part of the soul that survives does not flit about its new abode like a firefly; it has an inner body which it inhabits, and it is most natural that this body would resemble the human body of flesh and blood, though nothing like as gross, of course.

St. Paul was also asked the same question, and the pertinent verses of his reply may be found in 1 Corinthians 15:35/36, 42/44, 48/50, 53/57:

'But some men will say: How do the dead rise again? Or with that manner of body shall they come? Senseless man, that which thou sowest is not quickened, except it die first. .... So also is the resurrection of the dead. It is sown in corruption; it shall rise in incorruption. It is sown in dishonour; it shall rise in glory. It is shown in weakness; it shall rise in power. It is sown a natural body, it shall rise a spiritual body. If there be a natural body, there is also a spiritual body. .... Such as the earthly, such also are the earthly: and such as is the heavenly, such also are they that are heavenly. Therefore, as we have borne the image of the earthly, let us bear also the image of the heavenly. Now this I say, brethren, that flesh and blood cannot possess the kingdom of God; neither shall corruption possess incorruption. ..... For this corruptible must put on incorruption; and this mortal must put on immortality. And when this mortal hath put on immortality, then shall come to pass the saying that is written:

"Death is swallowed up in victory. O death, where is thy victory? O death, where is thy sting?" Now the sting of death is sin; and the power of sin is the law. But thanks be to God, who hath given us the victory through our Lord Jesus Christ.'

And in John 3:5/8, in answer to the question of Nicodemus on how a man can be born again, our Lord answered:

"Amen, amen, I say to thee, unless a man be born again of water and the Holy Ghost, he cannot enter the kingdom of God. That is which is born of the flesh is flesh; that which is born of the Spirit is spirit. Wonder not that I said to thee: You must be born again. The Spirit breatheth where he will and thou hearest his voice, but thou knowest not whence he cometh and whither he goeth. So is every one that is born of the Spirit."

There is a large and diverse amount of literature on this subject, but to turn again to the Catholic tradition, let us call to mind that when certain saints (and lesser visionaries) have seen and communicated with departed souls, they saw a human form, but one which most certainly was not of flesh and blood, and the glory and the light of this human form, or inner body, was in direct proportion to its purity and holiness. However, since many apparitions of such departed souls were in the context of their appealing for the prayers of the saint to whom they appeared, the condition of their inner bodies was anything but glorious. Many of us may have read of those incidents where a saint was asked to pray for a particular soul in purgatory, and the condition of that soul's inner body, as seen by the saint, before and after release from purgatory, was vastly different, one could say, like night and day, and even this would probably be a poor comparison.

To give another example of the existence of this inner body, in the biography on the life of St. Padre Pio, there is an incident where a monk who had been dead for many years appeared to him. Now it is clear that, in order to be recognisable, the departed soul must have had a human form, and since this form was not of flesh and blood, the soul must have inhabited an inner body like unto its physical body when it resided in this world.

A further example is the phenomenon of bilocation, or of a person being in two places at the same time. Padre Pio experienced this when he bilocated to another country to attend the deathbed of a fellow priest even though his physical body was in Italy at the time. Another incident may be quoted from the life of St. Martin de Porres, who had achieved such purity and holiness that it would seem his physical body was no impediment to his inner body, for when St. Martin was in haste to take a brazier of hot coals to warm a sick monk in another part of the monastery where he resided, he was seen to walk through solid walls, even while carrying the brazier. Many such incidents are described in religious literature, and it would be entirely unreasonable to deny all of them as superstitions hocus-pocus. Of course, one should not believe everything one either reads or hears about; sound judgment using our God-given reason is essential.

The question might now be asked, why, if God has no form, should the soul created by God exist in its heavenly abode subsequent to being purified in purgatory in a form like unto the form of the body it inhabited while living in the world? In answer to this, let us recall what St. John of the Cross said about the possibility of the soul becoming God by participation. Therefore, the closer the union of the soul with God, the more glorious its form, even though this form may still retain a human shape. Even in this life, the human form at its best has such great beauty and gracefulness (and why not, since it was created by God) that great artists have extolled it in their works of art, and we can all admire the expression of art that seems to transcend the limits of the human form that is depicted. Therefore, if from art we can appreciate the beauty inherent in the human form, how much more would we do so if we could understand that by denying ourselves and taking up our cross, we are creating a work of art of even greater beauty that reflects itself, not necessarily in our physical body, which is a subject to wear and tear and the ageing process, but in our inner body, in which dwell the higher faculties of the soul.

Unfortunately, the work of art of the soul as originally created by God has become badly tainted by sin. A skilled artisan can restore an ancient antique or a work of art to its original lustre, but it took the Passion of Christ to make possible the ultimate restoration of the soul to the condition its Creator intended. **And it is in the restoration of the inner body in which functions the superior part of the soul that I understand the above mentioned statement of St. Paul, when he referred to our resurrection as being a 'likeness' to that of the Resurrection of Christ.** And it is also in this manner that I understand the words from 1 Corinthians quoted above. Therefore, when certain priests and religious deny the Resurrection of Christ, they also deny the resurrection or restoration of the inner body and that of the superior part of the soul by the merits of the Passion of Christ. For this reason, they are justifiably described as 'wolves in sheep's clothing'.

Relative to what has been said above, the question may also be asked that if the Passion of Christ has redeemed our souls, then why should we have to go to purgatory to undergo purification? Should not the Passion have made the purification in purgatory unnecessary (this is the position of many non-Catholic Christians)? To answer this question, we should carry out a little self-introspection. How much (or better put, how little) do we in this life merit heaven? Do we deny ourselves anything that is in our power to acquire? To what degree have we become the 'Overcomer' referred to in the Apocalypse? How much time do we put in for personal prayer? Do we sacrifice a portion of our sleep for this purpose? Attending Mass and saying a few prayers while at Church is all right, but can hardly be called sacrificial. Let us consider what the saints have done in their lives, and then let us feel ashamed of our own paltry efforts. Our Lord knows our weakness, and how little we can contribute towards our own salvation.

Therefore the absolute necessity of His Passion to pay the price of our salvation; the justice of having to endure some time in purgatory for the purpose of the purification of our soul and inner body is an infinitesimal price to pay. We should not add insult to injury by implying that our Lord's Passion should also secure for us freedom from purgatory. We should also understand that we could not possibly appreciate our heavenly abode without first having gone through this purification.

As mentioned above, this essay will conclude with some brief comments on visions and locutions, why they cannot be understood in a literal manner, and how we can be deceived by them, even though they come from God, as for example, in the vision of the resurrection of dry bones in Ezekiel 37, which we maintained, could not be taken literally as an argument for the resurrection of the body of flesh and blood. As well as giving pertinent quotations from the Ascent, examples from Scripture will also be given.

In Book II, Chapter XIX of the Ascent, St. John of the Cross tells that:

'For two reasons we have said that although visions and locutions which come from God are true, and in themselves are always certain, they are not always so with respect to ourselves. One reason is the defective way in which we understand them; and the other, the variety of their causes. In the first place, it is clear that they are not always as they seem, nor do they turn out as they appear to our manner of thinking. The reason for this is that, since God is vast and boundless, He is wont, in His prophecies, locutions and revelations, to employ ways, concepts, and methods of seeing things which differ greatly from such purpose and method as can normally be understood by ourselves; and these are the truer and the more certain the less they seem so to us. This we constantly see in the Scriptures. To many of the ancients many prophecies and locutions of God came not to pass as they expected, because they understand them after their own manner, in the wrong way, and quite literally.'

St. John of the Cross then gives an example of where God tells Jacob: '...fear not to go down into Egypt. …..I will go down there with thee; and when thou goest forth thence again, I will bring thee out and guide thee.' But Jacob died in Egypt, and it was not until four hundred and thirty years later that Israel was brought out of Egypt [Genesis 46:3/4 and Exodus 12:40]

In the same Book and Chapter of the Ascent, St. John of the Cross gives a second example taken from Judges (which I somewhat abbreviate), where we read about the battle between the tribes of Israel and the tribe of Benjamin which took place in order to punish a certain evil that the tribe of Benjamin had consented to. Because God had appointed them (i.e. the tribes of Israel) a captain for the war, they were certain of victory. But they lost the initial battle quite badly. And when they enquired of God if they should give battle again or no, He answered that they should go and fight against the tribe of Benjamin. This time, they considered that the victory was to be theirs, and went out with great boldness, and were conquered again the second time. Thereat they were greatly confused, and knew not what to do, seeing that God had commanded them to fight and yet each time they were vanquished. And in this way, they were mistaken in their manner of understanding the words of God. St. John of the Cross continues: **'His words were not deceptive, for He had not told them that they would conquer, but that they should fight; for by these defeats God wished to chastise a certain neglect and presumption of theirs, and thus to humble them. But, when in the end He answered that they would conquer, it was so, although they conquered only after the greatest stratagem and toil.'**

In the same Book and Chapter, St. John of the Cross tells us that: '...in interpreting prophecy, we have not to consider our own sense in language, knowing that the language of God is very different from ours, and that it is spiritual language, very far removed from our understanding and exceedingly difficult......' He then relates how the Prophet Jeremias, when he saw that the significance of the words of God was so different from the sense commonly attributed to them by men, and was himself deceived by them, he defends the people, saying: 'Ah, ah, ah, Lord God, hast Thou perchance deceived this people and Jerusalem, saying, "Peace will come upon you", and seest Thou here that the sword reacheth unto their soul?' St. John of the Cross explains this by saying that: '......the peace that God promised them was that which was to be made between God and man by means of the Messiah Whom He was to send, whereas they understood it of temporal peace; and therefore, when they suffered wars and trials, they thought God was deceiving them, because there befell them the contrary of that which they expected......'

For the reasons given in the Book and Chapter referred to, St. John of the Cross stresses: '...... the necessity of dwelling in the liberty and darkness of faith, wherein are received spiritual liberty and abundance, and consequently the wisdom and understanding necessary to interpret the sayings of God. For it is impossible for a man, if he be not spiritual, to judge of the things of God or understand them in a reasonable way, and he is not spiritual when he judges them according to sense..... St. Paul well expresses in these words: "The animal man perceives not the things which are of the Spirit of God, for unto him they are foolishness and he cannot understand them because they are spiritual; but he that is spiritual judgeth all things [1 Cor. 2:14/15]." By the animal man is meant one that uses sense alone; by the spiritual man, one that is not bound or guided by sense. Wherefore it is temerity to presume to have intercourse with God by the way of a supernatural apprehension effected by sense, or to allow anyone else to do so.'

Also in Book II, Chapter XIX of the Ascent, St. John of the Cross gives an example of the difficulty in understanding the true import of prophecy:

'…..Let us suppose that the holy man is greatly afflicted because his enemies persecute him, and that God answers him, saying: "I will deliver thee from all thine enemies." This prophecy may be very true, yet, notwithstanding, his enemies may succeed in prevailing, and he may die at their hands. And so if a man should understand this after a temporal manner he would be deceived; for God might be speaking of the true and principal liberty and victory, which is salvation, whereby the soul is delivered, free and made victorious over all its enemies, and much more truly so in a higher sense than if it were delivered from them here below. And thus, this prophecy was much more true and comprehensive than the man could understand if he interpreted it only with respect to this life; for, when God speaks, His words are always to be taken in the sense which is most important and profitable, whereas man, according to his own way and purpose, may understand the less important sense, and thus may be deceived……'

To further illustrate what St. John of the Cross said in the preceding paragraph, I will quote from two examples in Scripture. In 4 Kings 22:20, King Josias was told by God that he would be gathered to his grave in peace, and that his eyes would not see all the evil that God would bring upon Jerusalem. However, in 4 Kings 23:29, when King Josias went to fight against the king of Egypt, he was killed in battle. The second example is taken from Luke 21:16/18, wherein in speaking to His disciples, Jesus said: 'And you shall be betrayed by your parents and brethren, and kinsmen and friends, and some of you they will put to death' [Luke 21:16]. However, in Luke 21:18, Jesus says: 'But a hair of your head shall not perish.' Now, it does not take much discernment to observe that these two verses are mutually contradictory if read literally; therefore, the verse quoted from Luke 21:18 cannot be understood literally.

There are numerous other passages in Scripture which would require enlightenment from God to understand, since they pertain to mysteries and secrets that certainly cannot be taken literally, and we cannot possibly understand them with our limited intellect. **We should also bear in mind that God speaks from the Eternal Present, whereas we are bound by time.** This principle is well exemplified by the few examples taken from Scripture, which follow:

Matthew 10: 23	'You shall not finish all the cities of Israel till the Son of man come.'
Matthew 16: 28	'There are some of them that stand here that shall not taste death, till they see the Son of man coming in His Kingdom.'
Matthew 24: 34	'This generation shall not pass, till all these things be done.'
John 8:51	'If a man keep my saying, he shall never see death.'
John 21:22	'Jesus said to Peter (talking about John): 'So I will have him to remain till I come, what is it to thee? Follow thou me.'
Apocalypse 2:11	'He that overcometh shall not be hurt by the second death.'
Apocalypse 20:6	'Blessed and holy is he that hath part in the first resurrection: on such the second death hath no power, but they shall be priests of God and of Christ and shall reign with him a thousand years.'
Apocalypse 20:14	'And death and hell were cast into the lake of fire. This is the second death.'

Although the meaning of such passages from Scripture would need to be revealed to us, we need only apply a little of our God-given common sense to dispel foolish interpretations. In Book II, Chapter XXII of the Ascent, in explaining the way that God usually deals with man, St. John of the Cross tells us that: 'For ordinarily, He neither performs nor reveals anything that can be accomplished by human counsel and effort. …..for He is ever desirous that men should make use of their own reason as is possible, and all such things have to be governed by reason, save those that are of faith, which transcends all judgment and reason, although these are not contrary to faith.'

Relative to the term **'second death'**, I am of the view that if all souls that have ever lived must undergo another judgment at the end of time, then this means that souls who had previously undergone the purification of purgatory and entered into heaven would be at risk of being one of the goats [Matt. 25:33], and those unfortunate souls who had previously ended up in hell would suffer double jeopardy, in that they would hardly merit being chosen as sheep, but at the very least would be sent back to where they came from, and even perhaps to a worse state than before. I think that we should not trouble ourselves about such mysteries as to what is meant by the **'second death'**, which would require great light from God to comprehend, but instead concentrate all our efforts in this life on ensuring that our first death will be a good one.

SOME COMMENTS ON THE ARTICLE - DEPOSIT OF FAITH AND THE PRIESTHOOD

I was only halfway through page one of the article when I became puzzled. I asked myself, 'What is the purpose of distributing this article to parishioners?' The meaning of the article itself became clear when I got to page 2. It is, in the main, a defence of the Faith written to combat the heresy of Modernism that has sapped the vitality of the dogma and doctrine of the Catholic Church over the years. It is interesting to note that this process started with academics, first in Germany, then in France, Italy and England. Such people have no spiritual life in them. There is now no country where this poison has not permeated. Therefore, we must ask ourselves why this should be. There must be, and is, a basic cause of which Modernism is but the effect. In my view, this cause is the lack of example among the clergy of the living of a truly holy life. Why is it that the people used to flock around the saints when they were alive? It was because of the living example of holiness (not just goodness) which emanated from them, and which like the flame of a candle, lit the wick of the lives of others. To excuse themselves from the necessary effort, clergy of the Modernist stamp argued that the saints were extraordinary in their self-denial and mortification, and it was not reasonable that ordinary men of the cloth should subject themselves to such 'extraordinary practices' without the grace that was clearly given to the saints. 'After all,' goes the argument, 'we are men like you!' This argument begs the question, which is: What should be the norm of a religious vocation? In my view, the people do not want men like them as religious. This attitude was the cause of so many young people flocking to India in the 1960's to seek a guru. They yearned for men who discernibly lived a higher life, disciplined examples who they could try to emulate. Unhappily, they did not always find it, but many were fortunate in finding someone who had made some progress in the spiritual life.

I do not believe it is sufficient to merely quote the Apostles of our Lord; one must look closely at the lives they led. And herein lies the reason why heresies like Modernism arise. It is because certain successors of the Apostles appear to have forgotten their true role. Here, it is appropriate to quote from Jeremias 23, verses 1 and 2: "Woe to the pastors that destroy and tear the sheep of my pasture, saith the Lord. Therefore, thus saith the Lord the God of Israel to the pastors that feed my people: You have scattered my flock and driven them away, and have not visited them: behold, I will visit upon you for the evil of your doings, saith the Lord."

The people are not fooled. Faith is not enough, especially in this modern age of technology, which is far more critical and disdainful of religious values than even the Age of Reason was in the 18th century. People in general need to see something work before they will commit themselves and change their somnolent attitude towards religion. But how does one communicate this to the masses? How does one place life within the seed of the Deposit of Faith? Clearly, this is the work of the Holy Spirit, but I do not think that religion should be restricted to the Deposit of Faith, which is a set of beliefs.

The Deposit of Faith is like a seed, which when planted, needs water and nourishment in order to flourish. Even the Holy Mass is not enough if it is not supplemented by principles of living by which the faithful conform their lives to the image of God within in order to be receptive to the reception of the Eucharist, so as to have the full benefit intended by its Giver. Year in and year out, people attend Holy Mass and receive the Eucharist, sometimes daily. Do we change? Are our lives an inspiration to our fellow man? This is a matter of observation. People are desperate to see holiness at work, even though today's pagan world seems to contradict this. If people do not worship God, they will worship something else.

Human nature abhors a vacuum. So today, we see people worshipping the world and all it has to offer to the senses. The Internet and the latest soap opera on television has more devoted adherents than religion probably ever had. So, unless religion can capture people's attention, they will remain captive to the outer, worldly things.

It is very difficult to get people to give up things which they value, even if such things are inimical to their souls, if they do not see examples before them to lead the way as personified by the leading representatives of the Church and the clergy. And herein lies the root of every heresy, the lack of example of the Deposit of Faith in the form of its Ministers. Even the older heresies, such as the Albigensian one, had its roots in this lack. Why were people who lived in the 13th century attracted to the representatives of the Albigensian heresy? It was because of their self-denial, their asceticism, which stood in stark contrast to the lives of the clergy at that time, notwithstanding their heretical teachings.

I am not suggesting that the clergy in general should become ascetics who fast and flagellate themselves (an interior flagellation is far more effective than an outward one), but what is required is a spirit and action of mortification that demonstrably sets them apart from ordinary men, and a dedication to the principles of religion which sets them apart from the world. God will not infuse virtues in us unless we first strive to acquire them. As Meister Eckhart said in his sermon on the twenty-first Sunday after Trinity Sunday: "We must not have virtues in our notebooks so that we only know and talk about them."

Truly speaking, there should be no difference, religiously speaking, between a "secular" priest (i.e. one who functions in the world) as opposed to one who is a religious bound by vows of poverty, chastity and obedience. Either a man is a true religious or he is not, and this applies equally to a lay person who is serious about his or her spiritual development. It is precisely this problem that is identified on page 3 of the article 'The Deposit of Faith and the Priesthood', where it distinguishes between so-called "Conservatives" and "Liberals", and refers to two different kinds of seminaries which prepare men for the priesthood. As the author of the article also points out, theology has lost its sacred character because it does not take its point of departure from the Articles of Faith. Although this has happened many times in the ebb and flow of human history, I do not believe that there has ever been a time, even during the persecutions of the past centuries, where the threat of total extinction of Catholic spirituality has been so close to a reality, to be replaced by a sort of scientific humanism. Here, we must recall our Lord's words, when He said to Peter: "You are the rock on which I will build my Church, and the gates of hell shall not prevail against it." Clearly, it looks like being a close call.

In order to restore the sacred character of Catholic spirituality, I am not advocating gloomy ascetics; it is possible to enjoy the innocent pleasures of the world and yet not place impediments to one's spiritual progress. As Johann Tauler said in one of his sermons for Pentecost, "It is not activity, but disordered activity that can hinder you. This you must avoid." One of the best guides on this difficult topic can be found in 'The Devout Life', which was written by St. Francis de Sales for one of his disciples who, due to her position in society, was forced to lead much of her life among the royalty in the French court at that time.

Protestantism has never been a threat to the progress of scientific humanism, because it has lost the vital element of the supernatural. It is Catholic Christianity that contains the supernatural aspects of the teachings of Jesus and which have been a vital part of the Catholic tradition down through the centuries. This tradition has become almost lost, because the supernatural aspect of religion, i.e. the intrinsic nature of the soul as the image of God and how the soul can develop a relationship with God, has become buried under the detritus of religious form without substance. Ultimately, it is in the hands of God to bring us to our senses, to a realisation of our true purpose in life, notwithstanding what we believe our priorities to be.

In the meantime, God does not desert us. Apart from the Saints, in every century there have been certain souls, sometimes very ordinary in their expressions of life, who have manifested in their lives the extraordinary of the supernatural in order to remind us that there is more to life than just eating, drinking, sleeping, having children and enjoying those things which appertain to the body. I am, of course, talking about genuine instances, proven over a long period of observation by their fruits and the practice of the virtues well above that of the ordinary person, and not just phenomena, and certainly not those numerous cases of hysterical obsession which afflict unbalanced personalities, or faked by those with a strong desire for attention. Unfortunately, for the most part, the Church appears to have ignored such souls, citing private revelation as the most common reason, or even fighting shy for the fear that Satan has a hand in such things.

However, by adopting this attitude, the Church ignores that private revelation is still 'revelation'. And while private revelation must always remain subservient to Public Revelation (i.e. the Scriptures), it is reasonable to conclude that genuine manifestations in which the hand of God brings the supernatural to our attention have a purpose, and are not just for the benefit of the souls so chosen, but are to be used under the direction of the Church in this age of gross materialism for the uplift and well-being of its members. The fact that this has not generally been the case does not obviate the duty of those responsible for the well-being of the body of the Church to look more closely at what God is doing in those genuine instances where He manifests the extraordinary. God does not waste His time, or bury a pearl in a field without desiring man to dig it up and assess its value.

In summary, The Deposit of Faith requires nourishment. The nourishment provided by Scripture, by the Mass and the reception of the Eucharist must be supplemented by an active development of the seed of the image of God within us if the intention of Jesus that His Body and Blood be Life indeed is to be realised in a practical way. While faith is an indispensable ingredient of this nourishment, many of us find it difficult to persevere by faith alone, since this requires leading a sacrificial and disciplined existence in a world that is unsympathetic to a life of sustained spirituality.

ON THE GREATNESS OF GOD AND THE LITTLENESS OF MAN

In his most excellent work, "Our Saviour and His Love for us", Fr. Reginald Garrigou-Lagrange, O.P., in the concluding chapter entitled "Mystics outside the Church", explains why true mystics are a rare phenomenon. I quote:

> "In conclusion, let us call to mind the reasons why true mysticism, although it is the normal blossoming of the life of grace, is, like perfect docility to the Holy Ghost, rare even in the visible Church. It is rare even in the religious orders, in spite of the assistance of the sacraments and in particular of daily Holy Communion. The mystical life is a normal development of the life of grace, but it is a lofty summit. Rarely do souls go beyond the fourth mansion, or prayer of quietude. The reason for this is that the mystical life ordinarily requires purity of heart, simplicity of mind, love of recollection, perseverance in prayer, and fervent charity, all of which are attainable when one makes the best use possible of the great means the Church provides; the sacraments, Holy Communion, and when one allows oneself to be molded by the liturgy and the supernatural study of sacred doctrine. This combination of conditions is not often realised even among Catholics, and therefore it is even less frequent among those who do not belong visibly to the Church."

In the same chapter, Fr. Garrigou-Lagrange says: "Let us not forget what St. John of the Cross says even of the most restricted Catholic circles. ....." He then refers to two works by this great saint: Dark Night of the Soul, and Living Flame of Love, and because the saint's comments in The Living Flame of Love are so appropriate, I reproduce them here:

"And here it behoves us to note the reason why there are so few that attain to this lofty state of the perfection of union with God. It must be known that it is not because God is pleased that there should be few raised to this high spiritual state, for it would rather please Him that souls should be perfect, but it is rather that He finds few vessels which can bear so high and lofty a work. For, when He proves them in small things and finds them weak and sees that they at once flee from labour, and desire not to submit to the least discomfort or mortification, He finds that they are not strong and faithful in the little things whereby He has granted them the favour of beginning to purge and fashion them, and sees that they will be much less so in great things; so He goes no further with their purification, neither lifts them up from the dust of the earth, through the labour of mortification, since for this they would need greater constancy and fortitude than they exhibit. And thus there are many who desire to make progress and constantly entreat God to bring them and let them pass to this state of perfection, and when it pleases God to begin to bring them through the first trials and mortifications, as is necessary, they are unwilling to pass through them, and flee away, to escape from the narrow road of life and seek the broad road of their own consolation, which is that of their perdition, and thus they give God no opportunity, refusing to receive what they have asked when He begins to give it to them. ……

Oh, souls that seek to walk in security and comfort in spiritual things! If ye did but know how necessary it is to suffer and endure in order to reach this security and consolation, and how without this ye cannot attain to that which the soul desires, but will rather go backward, ye would in no way seek consolation, either from God or from the creatures, but would rather bear the cross, and having embraced it, would desire to drink pure vinegar and gall, and would count this a great happiness, for being thus dead to the world and to your own selves, ye would live to God in the delights of the spirit; and bearing a few outward things with patience and faithfulness, ye would become worthy for God to set His eyes upon you, to purge and cleanse you more inwardly by means of more spiritual trials, and to give you more interior blessings. ….."

[Living Flame of Love- Second Redaction- Stanza II- Paragraphs 27/28 - Image Books- translated and edited by E. Allison Peers]

When He created us, God gave us a wonderful, yet fearsome gift, which is the gift of our free will. In many cases, the exercise of our free will is not subject to the pressure of our emotions, desires or habits, whether good or bad. But in much of our daily life, the opposite is true. I wrote on this subject in a previous essay "Some Thoughts on Free Will". On the last but one page of this essay, the references to one's right eye and right hand are symbols of our will and the importance of sacrificing our dearest possessions in the world if they prejudice our spiritual life. Most of us know how difficult it is to pluck out or cut off those things we hold most dear in this physical life. One can find examples in the lives of the saints, in which the things that were plucked out or cut off were sometimes members of their own families. Other examples may be found in the great prelates of the Church, such as St. Robert Bellarmine, who desired to give up his position as Cardinal and adviser to the Pope of his time in order to devote more time to his own spiritual development.

One cannot have one's cake and eat it too. In Scripture, we find the same advice:

"No man can serve two masters. For either he will hate the one and love the other: all he will sustain the one and despise the other. You cannot serve God and mammon." [Matthew 6:24]

"Enter ye in at the narrow gate: for wide is the gate and broad is the way that leadeth to destruction; and many there are who go in thereat.

How narrow is the gate and strait is the way that leadeth to life; and few there are that find it!" [Mathew 7:13/14]

The above verses apply not just to worldly people. There are many traps for those who consider themselves spiritual and teach others, yet do not learn themselves. For such, it is even more important that they spend more time in their own spiritual practices; otherwise, they will find themselves spiritually bankrupt.

I firmly believe that God, in His great compassion, never ceases to send us inspirations, contradictions, and helps of all sorts to deliver us. But what if we are not receptive to these inspirations? The inevitable result is that in the great majority of human actions, God's Will is not present. Our wills are so selfish, so fragile, so fickle, and so unstable, that they rarely, if ever, accord with the Will of God. This is why, in the Lord's prayer, Jesus asks us to pray that: "God's will be done on earth as it is in heaven". To put this into practice is the work of a lifetime, and I believe that we can say that we are making progress when we observe the numerous times when we do our own will and not the Will of God. The more we can identify the selfish motives of our own will behind what we do or say, the less likely are we to repeat our mistakes and the more likely to ask for God's Will to be done.

Many people will say to others (and themselves): I lead a good life, I pray every day, but nothing seems to change in my life. So what is the point of it all? I might as well do what is said in Ecclesiastes: "Therefore I commended mirth, because there was no good for a man under the sun but to eat, and drink and be merry; and that he should take nothing else with him of his labour in the days of his life, which God hath given him under the sun." (Ecclesiastes 8:15).

Apart from the fact that one must read the above scriptural verse in the context of Ecclesiastes as a whole, especially the last two verses of Chapter

12, the self-satisfied expression described in the preceding paragraph is a warning to all of us. What do people mean by 'leading a good life', and what is the quality of their prayer life? Here, let us reflect on some of the wonders and attributes of the Supreme Being we call God. We can observe some of these from the physical universe around us. On a bright, starry night, we can look up at the immensity of the night sky, filled with stars, only a fraction of which come within our gaze. We can have the greatest admiration for the discoveries of the astronomers, who by means of their observatories and radio telescopes, have greatly expanded man's knowledge of the physical universe, and even more, we can marvel at the power of the human brain, which allows man to create such inventions.

We can wonder at the spiritual insights granted to some favoured saints on the nature of the spiritual universe that can only be revealed to the soul, and which for the rest of humanity must remain a matter of faith. At our level, we can take delight in the beauty of the countryside, the seemingly infinite expanse of the oceans and the power of their waves. We can enjoy and appreciate the enormous variety of the foods that nourish our physical bodies, and wonder how God brought into being the seeds from which they grow. We can contemplate the existence of the animal kingdom, which has been placed at the service of mankind, and the teeming life of the oceans, which also provides a seemingly endless source of food for man.

All this and more we can think on to give us a faint idea of the grandeur, the power, and the attributes of God, and finally, we can marvel that Scripture and the science of the saints tell us that this Almighty God dwells within the deepest recesses of our souls, waiting with infinite patience for the opportunity to reveal Himself to us in those brief intervals when we think about Him, and when we seek Him within ourselves in sacrificial prayer.

Is it reasonable, then, to expect this glorious, infinite Being to reveal Himself without great effort and sacrifice being made to become receptive to His Presence within us? Is it not ridiculous to consider that an ordinary life and a few prayers are sufficient to attract His grace to enable us to participate in His endless glory? We can get a good idea of the effort and purity demanded of us from the quotes given above from the writings of the spiritual masters. And if we read their lives, we can take heart from the fact that they were men and women like us. No doubt they were given special graces, but to repeat what St Francis de Sales said, if we cannot follow them closely, we can do so at a distance.

Where there is a will, there is a way. If the great men of science, whose sacrifices and discoveries have made our lives so much easier, devoted their lives and intelligence to achieving worldly goals, why cannot we recognise what the intelligence and effort devoted by the saints in the spiritual realm have achieved! The great difference between the two is that the first is not lasting (this world will come to an end one day), while the second yields fruits for eternity.

Let us not be misled by certain clever scientists and mathematicians who, notwithstanding their wonderful discoveries, do not believe in God, but attempt to give a materialistic and rational explanation for the creation of the physical universe. Some of these theoreticians have come to the conclusion that throughout the universe a number of stars have collapsed internally, resulting in their gravitational fields becoming so dense that no matter or radiation can escape from them. They call this phenomenon "black holes". If such brilliant men believe that the physical universe just happened by chance, and that there is no Supreme Being behind its creation, then I conclude that there are more black holes in their brains than there are in the entire universe.

Scientists, whether or not they believe that God created the universe, have described the beginning of Creation by the theory of the 'Big Bang'. But this is not original, for in the 14th century, our Lord appeared to Julian of Norwich and showed her what appeared to be a hazelnut, lying in the palm of her hand, and she thought: "What can this be?" And she was given the general answer: "It is everything which is made." ['Showings' (Short text)- published by The Classics of Western Spirituality] It is not difficult to equate this description of Creation with the definition of the 'Big Bang', which is defined as: 'The rapid expansion of matter from a state of extremely high density' [Concise Oxford Dictionary].

Many people will agree with what has been said so far, but will ask what more can they do other than to lead a good, moral life. They will no doubt point out that the responsibilities of family life, of earning a living and coping with the stresses and demands of modern society leave them with little or no time for spiritual practices such as spiritual reading and prayer. My response to this is to remind such people of the value of time. St. Alphonsus De Liguori, a Doctor of the Church and the Founder of the Congregation of the Most Holy Redeemer, tells us that: "If we waste one minute of time, then that minute cannot be recaptured." He also quotes Seneca, a well-known philosopher of ancient Rome, who said that: "We have little time, because we lose a great deal of it."

In the times in which we live, these reminders become especially important because of the numerous and useless distractions that surround us. The principal culprits here are the television and the Internet. How many people are there, who every evening, put their feet up and turn on the television, saying to themselves, in one way or another, that: 'Now we can take things easy; we have earned this time of relaxation; there's no harm in it', and making similar convincing arguments in their minds. No doubt there are many things worth watching on television, but we should use our discrimination as to how far a legitimate desire for enjoyment and relaxation will affect our spiritual duty to our own soul. Regarding the Internet, how many are those who, instead of using it as a tool in this technological age, become captivated and spend hours roaming about from one site to another! Yes, the Internet is an excellent and powerful tool, but it is also a very bad master. I do not think it is a coincidence that the last three letters of this word form the word 'Net', and that the extensive information system used in conjunction with the Internet is called the 'World Wide Web'. It is well known that dolphins meet their death in the nets of fishing trawlers, and we all know what happens to the fly that gets caught in the spider's web.

The secret of living the spiritual life is the practice of prayer, mortification and the virtues, for it is this threefold practice that is the foundation of the spiritual life, and which leads us to union with God.

Someone has said: "Praying should be the most natural thing in the world. God didn't just make us and then walk off and leave us to it. He continually holds us in being, sustaining us every minute of the day. The life we live, every breath, and every movement is possible only because God continues to hold us, filling us with His Spirit and breathing life into us. God is closer to us than we can ever imagine -- He has built into us an intimacy with Him that is quite astonishing. We are already filled with God, we are already part of God. The natural expression of this bond between us and God is prayer. Prayer is our depths speaking to the depths of God. Through prayer we can share our joys and our sadness, finding refreshment and peace."

The question then arises, why do we find prayer so difficult if it should be natural to our being in relation to God's Being? The answer lies mostly in our will, and in the attention, which is directed by our will. Because we are in the body, which is in the world, our attention is continually dragged hither and thither, and our will, which seeks satisfaction through the outward expressions and enjoyments of the mind, finds prayer distasteful, since God can only be known within that deepest part of us wherein He resides. Most of us find it very difficult to 'interiorise', to find the centre of our being, because of the distractions of the mind which continually intervene. We usually begin our prayer life with the type of prayer which gives us satisfaction and which occupies the mind, such as vocal prayer or discursive meditation. But the saints tell us that to truly progress, we must go beyond these types of prayer to what is termed the prayer of recollection, silent prayer, or contemplative prayer. We are then led onward by God Himself. To aid us in this, the saints advise us to simplify our lives as much as possible and to practise mortification, which is nothing less than putting to death our lower nature.

The prayer that is recommended in the writings of the saints and other great souls is the prayer of recollection or internal prayer. In the words of St. Teresa of Avila, this consists of a shutting up of the faculties within itself by the soul. We must cast aside everything else, she goes on to say, in order to approach God inwardly, and we must retire within ourselves even during our ordinary occupations, and strive to ignore useless thoughts and the tyranny of our roaming imagination, which theologians have called the 'mad woman in the house'. The practice of the prayer of recollection will, by the grace of God, lead to what St. Teresa calls the Prayer of Quiet, which is the beginning of pure contemplation. She tells us that the Prayer of Quiet is a supernatural state, in which all the faculties are stilled. Scripture refers to this state in the following verses:

> "But when thou shalt pray, enter thy chamber, and having shut the door, pray to thy Father in secret, and thy Father who seeth in secret will repay thee." [Matthew 6:6]

> "And being asked by the Pharisees, when the kingdom of God should come? He answered them, and said: The kingdom of God cometh not with observation: Neither shall they say: Behold here, or behold there. For lo, the kingdom of God is within you." [Luke 17:20/21]

"Be still and see that I am God; I will be exalted among the nations, and I will be exalted in the earth." [Psalm 45:11]

In the Psalm, the nations represent our unruly thoughts and imagination, and the earth represents our desires and passions.

The practice of prayer must go hand in hand with practising mortification and developing the virtues, otherwise, as St. Teresa tells us, we shall never grow more than dwarfs. Four virtues mentioned in Scripture (the Book of Wisdom in the Old Testament) are Prudence, Justice, Fortitude and Temperance. They are known as the Cardinal Virtues, because they are the foundation of many other virtues. The gifts of the Holy Spirit are closely linked to the practice of the Cardinal Virtues. The well-known sayings of: 'Look before you leap', and 'Fools rush in where Angels fear to tread' are familiar examples of the Cardinal Virtue of Prudence.

To practise the virtue of temperance is also to practice mortification. In referring to prayer and mortification, St. Francis de Sales tells us:

"Interior and exterior mortification is a powerful means to draw down upon us the favours of heaven if we practice it in charity and through charity. Mortification without prayer is a body without a soul, and prayer without mortification is a soul without a body."

When we mortify our lower nature and practise internal prayer, we will observe that our dispositions change from the things of the world to those relating more to the state of our soul and to God; this is a sure sign of spiritual progress.

One of the most fruitful areas for practising mortification relates to the discipline of the palate. The capital sin of gluttony comes under this heading. If we cannot control our appetite, it will be impossible to control the other and much more difficult capital sins of pride, anger, lust, envy, and avarice.

The practice of mortification covers every unruly desire in our lower nature, and every sense in our human nature. Thus, in addition to that of the palate, or sense of taste, it includes restraining the senses of seeing, hearing, and touching from those things that can inflame the passions or desires; in a word, all of those things that can drag us out into the world, and make it difficult to practise the prayer of recollection. St John the Evangelist taught exactly these things when, in the First Epistle, he warns us about "the concupiscence of the flesh, the concupiscence of the eyes, and the pride of life." The word 'concupiscence' simply means 'unbridled or uncontrolled desire'.

We understand that the 'concupiscence of the flesh and the concupiscence of the eyes' have their seat in the lower part of the soul, while the 'pride of life' has its seat in the higher part of the soul, where our 'I-ness or ego' resides. Because these tendencies of our lower nature are so strong, and feed on useless thoughts and an uncontrolled imagination, it is essential that the practice of mortification must be both exterior and interior. If we strive to practise exterior mortification, we are more likely to be successful in mortifying the action of the mind. St. Alphonsus De Liguori gives more importance to interior mortification, for he says that: "External mortification, without interior self-denial, profits the soul but little." But he also says that: "It is true that interior mortification is the most necessary, but exterior mortification is also indispensable."

An indispensable aid to what has been said above is to devote some time to spiritual reading. The best form of spiritual reading is contained in those books where the writer speaks from experience; this we shall find in the lives and teachings of the saints and other great souls, either written by them or by their biographers. Books written by others, no matter how learned, will not have the same resonance within our souls. From experience, we shall find that we might read a book written by a learned man twice, or if it is a really spiritually nourishing book, even three times. But the books written by the saints can be read again and again; we can always gain something from each reading. The reason for this is that we have not attained to their spirituality, and therefore what we read is always fresh to us.

Spiritual reading continued throughout one's lifetime is essential to both understanding and developing the dispositions necessary to practise a life of prayer. Such reading gives an intimacy with the subject of spirituality that nothing else, other than a direct experience of the operation of God in our life can give. Attending talks or lectures on the subject can help; they can provide an impetus to our desire to know God, but they will soon fade from our memory unless we translate what we hear into positive action. In this regard, St. Augustine said in his Confessions:

"For it is one thing to see the land of peace from a wooden ridge ....
and another to tread the road that leads to it."

In conclusion, let us remember our last end. We are here for no other purpose than to prepare ourselves for the great change we call 'death'. How we do this depends on the use of that wonderful, yet fearsome gift of free will, and our responsibilities and activities in life are the means by which we prepare ourselves. God expects more from those who occupy positions of authority in life. He certainly expects more from those, who of their own free will, have chosen to serve Him in the religious life, such as priests and members of religious orders. But He expects no less from the ordinary man or woman in accordance with their station in life. To convince ourselves that the spiritual life is not something extraordinary, but in the words of St. John of the Cross, is in the normal way of sanctity to which we are all called, let us reflect on the beautiful and impassioned plea that this great saint and Doctor of the Church makes to souls near the completion of his work, the Spiritual Canticle:

"O souls created for these grandeurs and called thereto! What do you do? Wherein do ye occupy yourselves? Your desires are meannesses, and your possessions miseries. O wretched blindness of the eyes of your souls, which are blind to so great a light and deaf to so clear a voice, seeing not that for so long as ye seek grandeurs and glories ye remain miserable and mean, and have become ignorant and unworthy of so many blessings!"

We may not be resolute enough to take the words of this saint to heart 100%, but let us not ignore them altogether. It would be a most foolish thing to squander the opportunities we are given in this life to overcome our littleness in order to approach and unite with God's Greatness for eternity.

ON THE WORDS OF OUR LORD UTTERED IN THE GARDEN OF GETHSEMANI AND ON THE CROSS

To understand Jesus' cry of abandonment on the Cross: "My God! My God! Why hast thou forsaken Me?", one must link these words with His words in the Garden of Gethsemani, when He asked the Father to remove the cup from Him. This was the cup of the filth of sin of humanity, past, present, and future, that Jesus Christ took upon His human soul. As further explained below, this cup necessarily included mortal sin, and as the Church teaches, mortal sin results in the loss of Sanctifying Grace, that is to say, man cuts himself off from God.

Because the human soul of Jesus Christ the Son absorbed this cup of the filth of sin of humanity for a period of time unknown to us, be it a fleeting moment or longer, the Humanity of God the Son became separated from His Divinity on the Cross. It was this incomprehensible sacrifice that was the true sacrifice by which God the Son accomplished the Redemption of humanity, and this could only be done in the Incarnation, in which Christ the Son assumed a human soul. It is not possible for sin to touch the Divinity; therefore, in order to redeem humanity, the Second Person of the Trinity, the Word, perforce had to assume a human body and soul in order to accomplish the Redemption. So, contrary to the general understanding, it was not the physical aspect of the Passion of Christ, i.e. the scourging, the agony of the crown of thorns and the crucifixion, that was the true sacrifice, but the spiritual aspect, in which He took the sins of humanity upon His human soul.

This can be understood from Matthew 16:21/23 and Luke 12:50. In Matthew 16:21, Jesus tells His disciples that He must go to Jerusalem and suffer many things, and be put to death and on the third day, rise again. And when Peter said (Matthew 16:22): "Lord, be it far from Thee, this shall not be unto Thee.", Jesus responded (Matthew 16:23): "……Go behind me, Satan: thou art a scandal unto Me, because thou savourest not the things that are of God, but the things that are of men." And in Luke 12:50, Jesus tells us: "And I have a baptism wherewith I am to be baptised. And how am I straitened until it be accomplished." The modern meaning of the word 'straitened' is to be restricted; the archaic meaning is to 'make or become narrow', in other words, to be confined. Therefore, Jesus is telling us how held back, how eager He was, to accomplish the great sacrifice by which He was to redeem humanity. **But the part of His sacrifice that was most repugnant to Him was the drinking of the cup of the filth of sin, both mortal and venial sin, past, present and future, and this was why He asked the Father to remove it from Him.** This, we can understand from the words in Matthew 26:39, when He said: "My Father, if it be possible, let this chalice pass from me. Nevertheless, not as I will but as thou wilt." And again in Matthew 26:42 "My Father, if this chalice may not pass away, but I must drink it, thy will be done." By repeating the same request to the Father, which He knew could not be fulfilled, Jesus is telling us that it was this chalice (of the filth of sin of humanity) that was so repugnant to His Divinity. And so, in some mysterious fashion, God became not God, that is to say, the Humanity of Jesus became separated from His Divinity for a time, no matter how brief, when He assumed the sin of humanity on His human soul. **And this we can also understand from the teaching of the Church, in which we are told that mortal sin "…… results in the loss of charity and the privation of sanctifying grace, that is, of the state of grace. ……." (The Catechism of the Catholic Church, paragraph 1861).**

The understanding given above is based on the words of St. John of the Cross in his work the 'Ascent of Mount Carmel', Book II, Chapter VII, where he tells us:

"In the first place, it is certain that He died as to sense, spiritually, in His life, besides dying naturally at His death. For, as he said, He had not in His life where to lay His head, and at His death, this was even truer. In the second place, it is certain that, at the moment of His death, He was likewise annihilated in his soul, and was deprived of any relief and consolation, **since His Father left Him in the most intense aridity, according to the lower part of His nature. Wherefore He had perforce to cry out, saying: "My God! My God! Why hast Thou forsaken me?"** This was the greatest desolation, with respect to sense, that He had suffered in His life. **And thus He wrought herein the greatest work that He had ever wrought, whether in miracles or in mighty works, during the whole of His life, either upon earth or in Heaven, which was the reconciliation and union of mankind, through grace, with God.** And this, as I say, was at the moment and the time when this Lord was most completely annihilated in everything. Annihilated, that is to say, with respect to human reputation; since, when men saw Him die, they mocked Him rather than esteemed Him; and also with respect to nature, since His nature was annihilated when He died; and further with respect to the spiritual consolation and protection of the Father, since at the time He forsook Him, that He might pay the whole of man's debt and unite him with God, being thus annihilated and reduced as it were to nothing.

Wherefore David says concerning Him: "Ad nihilum redactus sum, et nescive" [Psalm 72:22 - And I am brought to nothing, and I knew not.]. This he said that the truly spiritual man may understand the mystery of the gate and of the way of Christ, and so become united with God, and may know that, the more completely he is annihilated for God's sake, according to these two parts, the sensual and the spiritual, the more completely is he united to God and the greater is the work which he accomplishes. And when at last he is reduced to nothing, which will be the greatest extreme of humility, spiritual union will be wrought between the soul and God, which in this life is the greatest and highest state attainable. This consists not, then, in refreshment and in consolations and spiritual feelings, but in a living death of the Cross, both as to sense and as to spirit ---that is, both inwardly and outwardly.

I will not pursue this subject farther, although I have no desire to finish speaking of it, for I see that Christ is known very little by those who consider themselves His friends: we see them seeking in Him their own pleasures and consolations because of their great love for themselves, but not loving His bitter trials and His death because of their great love for Him. I am speaking now of those who consider themselves His friends; for such as live far away, withdrawn from Him, men of great learning and influence, and all others who live yonder, with the world, and are eager about their ambitions and their prelacies, may be said not to know Christ; and their end, however good, will be very bitter. Of such I make no mention in these lines; but mention will be made of them on the Day of Judgment, for to them it was fitting to speak first this word of God, as to those whom God set up as a target for it, by reason of their learning and their high position.

But let us now address the understanding of the spiritual man, and particularly that of the man to whom God has granted the favour of leading him into the state of contemplation (for, as I said, I am now speaking to these in particular), and let us say how much such a man must direct himself toward God in faith, and purify himself from contrary things, constraining himself that he may enter upon this narrow path of obscure contemplation."

I AM AT A LOSS WHAT TO DO

"I am at a loss what to do". This is what we say when we have reached a point in life at which we truly do not know what to do, and when we have reached this point, we resort to desperate measures to try to resolve the difficulty. This is the position that God was in before He took the momentous step of becoming Man in order to save humanity from itself. Here, it is interesting to note that this was not the first time that humanity had reached such a point of degradation that warranted its destruction, where it had fallen so low from the image of God in which it was created (Genesis 1:27). For, in the ancient past, we are told in the Book of Genesis that: 'And God, seeing that the wickedness of men was great on earth, and that all the thought of their heart was bent upon evil at all times, it repented him that he had made man on earth. And being touched inwardly with sorrow of heart, He said: 'I will destroy man, whom I have created, from the face of the earth…..for it repenteth me that I have made them.' (Genesis 6: 5/7). And so it happened, for mankind as it then existed was destroyed in the Flood, and only a remnant was saved, as related in the story of Noe (or Noah) and the Ark.

And because history has a tendency to repeat itself, the falling away from God and His Laws by generations subsequent to the Flood brought humanity to the same brink of destruction. So why did God not destroy humanity as before? Again, we must look to Scripture for the answer, for after Noe had built an altar to the Lord and offered sacrifices upon it, we are told: 'And the Lord smelled a sweet savour, and said: I will no more curse the earth for the sake of man: for the imagination and thought of man's heart are prone to evil from his youth: therefore I will no more destroy every living soul as I have done.' (Genesis 8:21)

So what was God to do? He was faced with the reality of man's sinful nature, because of which a falling away from the worship of God and obedience to His Laws brought mankind to the same position as it was prior to the Flood, and He was also bound by His own stricture that He would no more destroy every living soul. In this regard, we have only to read the words of Moses in Chapter 28 of the Book of Deuteronomy of the blessings that those who keep the commandments of God would receive and the curses that would come upon those who don't. And we also read that the prophecy of Moses was fulfilled as to the curses when the subsequent generations of the Jewish people fell away from those commandments, which culminated in their final dispersion in the time of the Romans in A.D. 70, which was foretold in Deuteronomy, chapter 28, verse 64. And it was seventy years before this took place that the promised Messiah was born, and this was the event that is referred to above in the first paragraph, where it is stated that God took the momentous step of becoming Man in order to save future humanity from itself, and this He did when He took the cup of the filth of sin of humanity, past, present and future, upon His human soul, as related in the Gospel of St. Matthew, Chapter 26, which culminated in His death on the Cross, as related in Chapter 27. [I have written on the Sacrifice of Christ in greater detail in the essay: "On the Words of our Lord uttered in the Garden of Gethsemani and on the Cross".]

It is also highly instructive to read verses 15 and 19 of Chapter 30 and verses 15 and 29 of Chapter 32 of Deuteronomy:

'Consider that I have set before thee this day life and good, and on the other hand, death and evil. .....I call heaven and earth to witness this day, that I have set before you life and death, blessing and cursing. Choose therefore life, that both thou and thy seed may live.' (Verses 15 and 19 of Chapter 30). 'The beloved grew fat, and kicked: he grew fat, and thick and gross. He forsook God who made him: and departed from God his saviour. .....O that they would be wise, and would understand, and would provide for their last end.' (Verses 15 and 29 of Chapter 32).

Verse 15 of Chapter 32 describes our present times to perfection.

No doubt there are many who have studied the changes that have taken place over the centuries, especially in regard to the laws and the punishments for breaking them that are set out in the Old Testament and in the New Testament for the most serious moral offences (especially sexual ones), as proof that, since these changes have not attracted Divine punishment, then these laws and punishments were really man-made, and did not have Divine authority. This argument is not unreasonable, but it ignores the fact that such laws and related punishments (which I certainly believe were given to Moses by God) were fitting for the times to which they applied. To lessen the severity of punishments for certain offences is one thing; to do away with them altogether and to effectively adopt the position that anything goes is quite another.

When we read Leviticus 18:22 and 20:13, Deuteronomy 22:5, 3 Kings 14:24, and Romans 1:26/27, it is clear that the act most offensive to God and that eventually brought about His Justice, relates to homosexuality. Now, given that mankind has offended God in so many ways, and that homosexuality has existed from ancient times to our present times, why should this be? Again, we must seek the answer in Scripture. In Genesis 1:27, we read:

'And God created man to his own image; to the image of God he created him. Male and female he created them.'

And in speaking of the institution of marriage, Genesis 2:24 tells us: **'Wherefore a man shall leave father and mother, and shall cleave to his wife; and they shall be two in one flesh.'**

The verse quoted from Genesis 1:27 tells us in the clearest possible language of the priceless value of our souls. Regrettably, we have only to read the verses quoted above from Chapters 30 and 32 of Deuteronomy to see how humanity has, by and large, rejected its divine destiny. I don't think that God expects most of us to reach the heights of sanctity achieved by the saints, but He does expect us to obey His just and righteous laws and to strive for holiness to the best of our ability and in accordance with our state in life as much as we possibly can. And if we do this, He will do the rest and make up for our shortcomings after we leave this life. But the sin He cannot tolerate is the one that destroys the image of God within us. And when we speak of sin, I think we must understand it as **putting into practice the evil within us, and not just the tendencies or temptations we have to do so**. It is by resisting the thoughts and tendencies that spring from our lower nature that we gain spiritually, and it is by putting them into practice that puts us on the road to a state of hell. And the worst sins that destroy the image of God within us are those which relate to improper sexual behaviour. In my essay "On Adam and Eve", I have developed this theme further. I would also refer my readers to paragraphs 2357 to 2359 of the Catechism of the Catholic Church. In this regard, paragraphs 2358 and 2359 are so appropriate that I quote them here:

> "The number of men and women who have deep-seated homosexual tendencies is not negligible. This inclination, which is objectively disordered, constitutes for most of them a trial. They must be accepted with respect, compassion and sensitivity. Every sign of unjust discrimination in their regard should be avoided. These persons are called to fulfill God's will in their lives and, if they are Christians, to unite to the sacrifice of the Lord's Cross the difficulties they may encounter from their condition.
>
> Homosexual persons are called to chastity. By the virtues of self-mastery that teach them inner freedom, at times by the support of

disinterested friendship, by prayer and sacramental grace, they can and should gradually and resolutely approach Christian perfection."

But here, I will be told that this has been the case throughout the history of humanity. If God wants to make His image within us a reality, why did He make it so difficult? After all, sexual desire is part of our human nature, and if He created our lower human nature as well as His image within our soul, we need to be saints in order to become the Overcomer referred to in chapters 2, 3 and 21 of the Apocalypse, the last Book in the Bible. But the answer to this is that God has given us the tools to become the Overcomer, to sublimate our lower human nature into the Divine nature by practising the virtues and using the power inherent in the faculty of our will to put them into practice. If we choose not to do so, we cannot blame God for this. Perhaps He doesn't expect us to rise to the height of sanctity of His saints, but He does expect us to obey His just laws as given in Scripture, as stated above. And here, it is appropriate to point out that the worst sin of our modern times, one that was not committed in past ages, is that much of Society has seen fit to pass legislation that permits people of the same sex to marry, an act that must be most offensive to God and that flies in the face of what we have been told in Genesis 1:27 and 2:24 quoted above. **It is as though man has thrown down the gauntlet before the face of God, challenging Him to a duel, saying: 'See, we have broken Your most sacred law; what are You going to do now?'**

So, what is God going to do now? Although God is bound by His promise and He will no more destroy every living soul, we should focus on the word "every". What more can He do for humanity than He has done, by assuming a human body and soul in order to carry out His sacrificial act as described above? What is He to do now that humanity has, by and large, thrown His sacrifice back in His face?

The attitude of today's world can be summarised by the following statement: "We are living in the modern world; what relevance is there to us on what took place over two thousand years ago? Today, we have the use of inventions such as television, the Internet, smartphones, and other marvellous creations of man. We have outgrown the religious superstitions of ancient times." So goes the argument of much of the world and its leaders. Well, if things go on as they have, and there is little doubt that they will, we shall most certainly find out what the response of God will be to this attitude. And if we want a preview, all we need to do is to read the following verses of Chapter 24 of the Gospel of St. Matthew. Much of this chapter is prophetic and full of warnings, and I quote below those verses, which to my mind apply to the times we are living in:

Verses 1 and 2: 'And Jesus being come out of the temple, went away. And his disciples came to shew him the buildings of the temple. And he answering, said to them: Do you see all these things? Amen I say to you, there shall not be left here a stone upon a stone that shall not be destroyed.'

Verse 12: 'And because iniquity hath abounded, the charity of many shall grow cold.'

Verse 14: 'And this gospel of the kingdom shall be preached in the whole world, for a testimony to all nations; **and then shall the consummation come.**'

Verses 21/22: 'For there shall be then great tribulation, such as hath not been from the beginning of the world until now, neither shall be. And unless those days had been shortened, no flesh should be saved: but for the sake of the elect those days shall be shortened.'

Verses 38/39: 'For, as in the days before the flood they were eating and drinking, marrying and giving in marriage, even till that day in which Noe entered into the ark: And they knew not till the flood came and took them all away: so also shall the coming of the Son of man be.'

Only a fool would ignore the import of verses 21/22 quoted above. Clearly, they relate to the "end times", and looking at the state of the world today, one cannot help but wonder how close we are to them. In their unwisdom, governments have completely set aside the moral laws in the Bible, and to put matters bluntly, anything goes. As mentioned above, the incomprehensible sacrifice of Jesus Christ, in which He took the sin of humanity, past, present and future, upon His human soul, has been literally thrown back in His face. However, it is heartening to read in verse 22 above that some of the "elect" will be living at the time when the hand of the Justice of God the Father will fall upon humanity. And by the word "elect" is meant, I believe, not just those who have achieved great sanctity in their lives, but ordinary people who still have faith in God and who strive to live a good, holy life.

To return to the title of this essay: **"I am at a loss what to do"** cannot of course be said of God. But it does highlight His almost inexhaustible patience and mercy, which has been so taken for granted as to give rise to the widespread but false belief that the truths of religion are not really truths, but are a system of antiquated superstitious beliefs that were the product of the times in which they appeared. No doubt this was also the view of many prior to the destruction of Jerusalem and the final dispersion of the Jewish people nearly two thousand years ago. They should have listened to their prophets, but they didn't. They should also have taken to heart the expression "The Day of the Lord", of which they were warned in the prophecies of Isaias, Joel, Amos, Abidas, Sophonias, Zacharias and Malachias, but they didn't. And the same errors, and even worse, are being made in our times. Here, I shall quote just a couple of texts from the Book of the Prophet Isaias, in which the expression "The Day of the Lord" appears:

'Howl ye, **for the day of the Lord is near**; it shall come as a destruction from the Lord. Therefore shall all hands be faint, and every heart of man shall melt.' (Isaias 13:6/7)

'Behold, **the day of the Lord**' shall come, a cruel day, and full of indignation, and of wrath and fury, to lay the land desolate, and to destroy the sinners thereof out of it.' (Isaias 13:9)

I will share one more verse, which tells us in a most beautiful, but absolutely clear way, how mankind has, over the centuries, spurned the commandments and just laws of God, as given through the agency of His prophets. And still we do not listen. It is taken from the Book of the Prophet Ezekiel.

'**And thou art to them as a musical song, which is sung with a sweet and agreeable voice: and they hear thy words and do them not. And when that which was foretold shall come to pass (for behold it is coming), then shall they know that a prophet hath been among them.**' (Ezekiel 33: 32/33)

MY LAST WORD

"Hey diddle diddle, the cat and the fiddle,
the cow jumped over the moon;
the little dog laughed to see such fun,
and the dish ran away with the spoon."

An English Nursery Rhyme of many years ago. But I think that it has much relevance to the times in which we live. Why do I say this? Because people living in today's world have, by and large, forgotten their true destiny, that we were created in the image of God (Genesis 1:27), and that the true purpose of life is to develop this image to the best that we can in this life. I have written on this theme in other essays. Instead of this noble purpose, so many live their lives like the cat, the cow and the little dog in the above nursery rhyme, so busy with their smartphones and apps, and the time-wasting things of which the Internet and television are full of, and they end up like the dish that ran away with the spoon, i.e. the dish of their soul remains empty, so its spoon has nothing to offer God at the time of their death.

To further put the above nursery rhyme into a modern perspective, today, we don't worship sticks and stones made by the hand of man; but as mentioned above, we have other, more sophisticated idols such as the Internet, smartphone, television and other electronic playthings. We all know where we stand in relation to them. This is not to say that we should not make use of these modern inventions (I am not a Luddite), but how many of us use them as one would a useful tool instead of frittering much of our time away in useless pursuits? Such things can be a good servant, but they are most certainly a bad master. We forget what the great Italian saint, St Alphonsus Liguori, the founder of the Redemptorist Religious

Order, told us. He said that if we waste just one minute of our time on earth, we can never recapture it.

In a previous essay, entitled "The Impact of Events in the Middle East on World History", I referred to a book written by Monsignor Eugene Kevane, Ph.D., a Catholic priest; the title of this book is "The Deposit of Faith: What the Catholic Church Really Believes." In this book, the author tells us that Pope St Pius X, being full of awareness of the general evils of the day, rooted in the religious ignorance of so many nominal Catholics, addressed this question in his first Encyclical "On the Restoration of All Things in Christ" (October 4, 1903), in which he says:

> "Who can fail to see," he writes, "that at the present time society is suffering more than in any past age from a terrible and radical malady which, while developing every day and gnawing into its very being, is dragging it to destruction?.... There is good reason to fear that this great perversity may be the foretaste and perhaps the very beginning of those evils reserved for the last days, and the 'son of perdition' of whom the Apostle speaks, may already be in the world."

The above Encyclical was written many years ago, and we could ask ourselves the question: What would Pope Pius X say today? Of course, we cannot know the answer, but there are significant Scriptures that can be quoted on the danger that faces mankind, which in my opinion, give us the answer, and I shall quote certain of these below, after which I shall set out my understanding of them.

> "And the earth is infected by the inhabitants thereof: because they have transgressed the laws, they have changed the ordinance, they have broken the everlasting covenant. Therefore shall a curse devour the earth: and the inhabitants thereof shall sin. **And therefore they that dwell therein shall be mad: and few men shall be left.**" [Isaias 24:5/6]

"And this shall be the plague wherewith the Lord shall strike all nations that have fought against Jerusalem: **the flesh of every one shall consume away while they stand upon their feet, and their eyes shall consume away in their holes, and their tongue shall consume away in their mouth.**" [Zacharias 14:12]

"And the shapes of the locusts were like unto horses prepared unto battle. And on their heads were, as it were, crowns like gold: and their faces were as the faces of men. And they had hair as the hair of women: and their teeth were as lions. And they had breastplates as breastplates of iron: **and the noise of their wings was as the noise of chariots and many horses running into battle. And they had tails like to scorpions: and there were stings in their tails.** And their power was to hurt men five months. ……." [The Apocalypse 9:7/10]

"**And the number of the army of horsemen was twenty thousand times ten thousand.** And I heard the number of them." [The Apocalypse 9:16]

"And thus I saw the horses in the vision. And they that sat on them had breastplates of fire and hyacinth and of brimstone. **And the heads of the horses were as the heads of lions: and from their mouths proceeded fire and smoke and brimstone.** ……." [The Apocalypse 9:17]

"**For the power of the horses is in their mouths and in their tails. For their tails are like to serpents and have heads: and with them they hurt.**" [The Apocalypse 9:19]

"And the sixth angel poured out his vial upon that great river Euphrates and dried up the water thereof, **that a way might be** prepared for the kings from the rising of the sun." [The Apocalypse 16:12]

"For there shall be then great tribulation, such as hath not been from the beginning of the world until now, neither shall be. **And unless those days had been shortened, no flesh should be saved: but for the sake of the elect those days shall be shortened."** [Matthew 24:21/22]

"And he laid hold on the dragon, the old serpent, which is the devil and Satan, and bound him for a thousand years. [Verse 2 of chapter 20 of The Apocalypse] And he cast him into the bottomless pit and shut him up and set a seal upon him, that he should no more seduce the nations till the thousand years be finished. **And after that, he must be loosed a little time.** [Verse 3 of Chapter 20] ..... And when the thousand years shall be finished, Satan shall be loosed out of his prison and shall go forth and seduce the nations which are over the four quarters of the earth, Gog and Magog: and shall gather them together to battle, **the number of whom is as the sand of the sea."** [Verse 7 of Chapter 20]

"And he shall destroy in this mountain the face of the bond with which all people were tied and the web that he began over all nations. He shall cast death down headlong for ever. And the Lord God shall wipe away tears from every face. And the reproach of his people he shall take away from off the whole earth. For the Lord hath spoken it." [Isaias 25:7/8]

"And I saw a new heaven and a new earth. For the first heaven and the first earth was gone: and the sea is now no more. ..... And God shall wipe away all tears from their eyes: and death shall be no more. Nor mourning, nor crying, nor sorrow shall be any more: for the former things are passed away. And he that sat on the throne said:

Behold, I make all things new. And he said to me: Write. For these words are most faithful and true." [The Apocalypse 21:1,4,5]

Before I make some brief comments on the Scriptural quotes given above, it is necessary to make an observation on prophecy in general. First, most prophecies cannot be understood literally. Communications from God take place in the Timeless, whereas we are bound by time and many other limitations. This is one reason why we find apocalyptic prophecies of destruction in chapter 24 of Isaias followed by a prophecy of the restoration of humanity in chapter 25 of Isaias. In this regard, the Book of the Prophet Isaias follows the same pattern as that of the Apocalypse of St. John. Indeed, to stretch the point I am making even further, we must read each verse in Scripture as though it were a chapter in itself. For example, verses 9/13 of Chapter 13 of Isaias, which prophesy events of cataclysmic proportions, seem strangely out of place in the chapter as a whole unless we read the reference to "Babylon" in Chapter 13 as a figure of modern-day Babylon (i.e. the modern world as we know it) as well as a reference to Babylon in the days of the Prophet Daniel. **To conclude these general comments, one must recognise that the language of Scripture, especially in the case of visions, is highly symbolic in nature. Also, that one who experiences them is in a very different state of consciousness that I have referred to above as the "Timeless".**

Comments

The words in bold type in the quote from Isaias 24:5/6 can certainly be linked to the words in bold type in Matthew 24: 21/22. The word "elect" in Matthew 24:22 does not, in my opinion, refer to saints, but to those who still have a strong faith in God in the materialistic, atheistic times in which we now live, and who would be living in the times referred to in Matthew 24. In Zacharias 14:12 (which should be read in context with Matthew 24), there is only one event that the words in bold type describe, and this is what would happen if a hydrogen bomb were to be dropped on the population of a particular country. And I think that this is what the Prophet Zacharias saw when he was taken into the Timeless, where there is no time, but only the eternal present. Here, I would note that both Zacharias and the Prophet Daniel lived in the times of King Cyrus, a little more than two thousand, five hundred years ago, I believe.

In verses 7/10 of Chapter 9 of the Apocalypse, with a little imagination, one can identify the 'locusts' as the warplanes of World War II. Although verses 4 and 5 of Chapter 9 are difficult to reconcile with verses 7/10, the time referred to of 'five months' in verse 5 is not one such difficulty, because one cannot be certain that when a specific period, e.g. a month or day, is referred to in Scripture, how long that period actually is. Indeed, the reference to 'five months' in verse 5 can be interpreted as five years, which was the duration of World War II. In interpreting verses 7/10 of Chapter 9, I have an advantage over most of my readers, since when I was a boy growing up in London during the war, I saw these 'locusts'. It is not hard to envisage the nose of a plane as part of a human face. And the exhaust vapour streaming out from the rear of a plane certainly resembles the hair of women. It may also be noted that American airmen who came over to England during the War often painted the faces of women on their planes. The 'stings in the tails' mentioned in verse 10 could either be the tail gunner or the bombs coming from beneath a plane, or both.

In verses 17 and 19 of Chapter 9 of The Apocalypse, St. John described what he called "horses that had heads of lions: and from their mouths proceeded fire and smoke and brimstone" (verse 17), and "For the power of the horses is in their mouths and in their tails. For their tails are like to serpents and have heads: and with them they hurt" (verse 19). In these two verses, one can envisage the revolving gun turret of a tank or other heavy armoured vehicle.

It is close to two thousand years ago that St. John had his visions of these modern-day weapons of war, and I consider that it was perfectly natural that he would have described an airplane as a locust and a tank as a horse, for there would have been no other vocabulary available to him in his day to describe such things.

The quotes from The Apocalypse, verse 16 of Chapter 9 and verse 12 of Chapter 16, are linked. When we multiply the two numbers mentioned in verse 16 of Chapter 9, we get two hundred million. Now, I think that there is only one country in the world that could muster such a huge army, and this is the same country that is referred to in the words in bold type in verse 12 of Chapter 16 of The Apocalypse. It would also seem that the words in bold type in verse 7 of Chapter 20 of The Apocalypse refer to the same country. It is a country that does not believe in God, and if a small portion of its population avow their belief in Christ Jesus, it is only tolerated by the government of this country. I leave it to the reader to determine the name of that country; this should not be too difficult.

In verse 2 of Chapter 20 of The Apocalypse, the binding of Satan for a thousand years stands for the millennium of the Church that commenced in the fourth century following the conquest by Emperor Constantine (the first Christian Emperor) and began to decline in the sixteenth century. The words in verse 3 of Chapter 20: "And after that, he must be loosed a little time", and the words in verse 7 of Chapter 20: "And when the thousand years shall be finished, Satan shall be loosed out of his prison and shall go forth and seduce the nations which are over the four quarters of the earth...." refer to the time of the Antichrist. In this connection, see above where I refer to the book The Deposit of Faith written by Monsignor Eugene Kevane and the words of Pope St. Pius X. There is not the slightest doubt in my mind that we are now living in these times (known as the "end times"), and barring a miracle, I believe that things can only get worse.

Verses 7 and 8 of Chapter 25 of Isaias and verses 1,4 and 5 of Chapter 21 of The Apocalypse speak for themselves. They are a tonic for those of us who still have faith in our Lord Jesus Christ, God the Son. On this positive note, I bring this essay to a close.

ON THE UNDERSTANDING OF CERTAIN HARD SAYINGS IN MATTHEW 5:39/42

Matthew 5 contains the Beatitudes and other verses that are not only difficult to comprehend, but most certainly hard to follow in our day-to-day lives. This essay is an attempt to clarify verses 39/42, which tell us:

"[39] But I say to you not to resist evil: but if one strike thee on thy right cheek, turn to him also the other: [40] And if a man will contend with thee in judgment and take away thy coat, let go thy cloak also unto him. [41] And whosoever will force thee one mile, go with him other two. [42] Give to him that asketh of thee: and from him that would borrow of thee turn not away." [Douay-Rheims Bible.]

In the foregoing verses, our Lord is clearly telling us that this is what He does for us. In putting up with our obstinacy, He is constantly offering His left cheek to be struck; He is constantly permitting Himself to be stripped of His rights when we spurn His commandments; He is constantly going the extra mile with us in waiting for us to change. And whenever we ask for forgiveness of our sins, He never withholds His mercy and grace.

Verses 39/42 are also examples of those virtues which only the most perfect saints, such as St. Francis of Assisi, can put into practice. This of course, also applies to many other commandments in Scripture. As I pointed out in a previous essay (On Adam and Eve), the Holy Bible contains four meanings: (i) the literal (ii) the moral (iii) the allegorical, and (iv) the anagogical or hidden, mystical meaning. The verses quoted above partake of all four.

The teaching of our Lord in Matthew 5 is mainly addressed to two groups within society. First, those who have chosen to follow the religious life, but especially those who have chosen the monastic life in religious orders, and second, those of us who live in this world and who wish to live our religious life seriously by mortifying our lower nature and practising prayer, especially the prayer of recollection, also known as contemplative prayer.

Christ Himself exemplified the first group when He came before Pontius Pilate, and uttered not a word in reply to the accusations brought against Him, so that Pilate himself wondered exceedingly. As an example of how the saints followed our Lord's advice to the first group, I quote the following story taken from the life of St. Francis de Sales, which illustrates one of the most difficult of Christian precepts, that of love towards one's enemies. It is taken from the book 'A Year with the Saints', published by Tan Books, Rockford, Illinois:

"A lawyer who lived in Annecy hated the holy prelate for no visible cause and was constantly speaking ill of him, injuring and persecuting him, so that he even tore down one of his notices which was fastened upon the church door and scrawled a thousand disgraceful figures on his confessional. The saint, who knew all this, met him one day and made him a friendly bow; then taking him by the hand with great politeness, he said whatever he thought most likely to make him change his course; but seeing that his words produced no effect, he added: 'I clearly perceive that you hate me, though I do not know why. But assure yourself that if you were to put out one of my eyes, I would look at you with the other as amicably as if you were my best friend.' The man's heart, however, was not softened by this, nor by the efforts of his friends to lead him to reconsider his actions. On the contrary, after firing pistol shots at his windows, he one day fired at the Bishop himself in the street, but by mistake wounded his vicar. For this act he was imprisoned by the senate, and notwithstanding the interposition of the saint, he was condemned to death. But the holy Bishop, having obtained a reprieve, used his influence with the king so successfully as to obtain his pardon. He went himself to the prison to bring the good news, and to entreat him to abandon a hostility for which he had no just cause. Finding him hardened as ever and ready with calumnies and insults, he knelt and asked his pardon. Finally, perceiving that nothing would move him, he left by his side the pardon he had obtained for him and took leave, saying: 'I have rescued you from the hands of man's justice, and you are not converted. You will fall under the justice of God, from which you cannot escape.' This soon happened; for a little while after, his life came to an unhappy end."

The story of the unfortunate man who would not listen to St. Francis de Sales can also be illustrated by the following saying of St. Augustine:

"God created us without us, but He will not save us without us."

We can paraphrase the saying in the following terms: "God has no mind to change a man who has no mind to change himself", or "The only person who can change a person is that person himself. With God's help of course."

Turning now to those of us who are in the second group, few, if any, would offer our left cheek to one who strikes us on the right cheek (verse 39), or would let ourselves be stripped of our assets in an unlawful lawsuit (verse 40). And who is there that would, if forced to go one mile with someone (i.e. put up with their unreasonable demands), go with them for another two (i.e. give that person everything he wanted)? (verse 41). And while we might wish to be charitable with certain persons, I don't think that we would lend to everyone who wanted to borrow from us. In this regard, I don't believe it is forbidden for those of us in the second group to use prudence and discretion, especially in the world that we are living in today (verse 42).

In Matthew 18:15/17, Christ also gave an example for the second group when He said:

> "But if thy brother shall offend against thee, go and rebuke him between thee and him alone. If he shall hear thee, thou shalt gain thy brother. And if he will not hear thee: take with thee one or two more, that in the mouth of two or three witnesses, every word may stand. And if he will not hear them: tell the church. And if he will not hear the church: let him be to thee as the heathen and publican."

As a final comment, and to prevent any misconception of what has been said above, although the term "the second group" refers to those who, regardless of their religion, wish to live their faith seriously, God calls all to seek Him and live according to His commandments. This is made abundantly clear in the words of Deuteronomy 6:5, which tell us that: "Thou shalt love the Lord thy God with thy whole heart, and with thy whole soul, and with thy whole strength." Which is to say, all are called to belong to the second group. This is the true purpose of our life on earth. However, as I pointed out in two of my other essays: "I am at a loss what to do", and "My last Word", I think that time is running out.

UNITY OF MAN

The following article was written in 1974 in Toronto, Canada, at the request of my wife. My wife was in India at that time, being asked to return by Sant Kirpal Singh, President of the World Fellowship of Religions, for the purpose of coordinating the arrangements for the many guests who would be arriving in Delhi, India, to attend a major conference, which included a conference on the 'Unity of Man'. There was an essay competition on this topic, and I was asked to submit my thoughts on what 'Unity of Man' meant and how it could be achieved. The article that I wrote in 1974 follows.

There are many problems facing mankind today of a social and political nature, but at their root is the fundamental problem from which all others arise. This problem is spiritual in its nature, and the analysis that follows is an attempt to explain it in terms that can be related to all other social and political ills from which the world suffers today.

If we look around the world at the present time, we observe that the lack of unity that exists would be hard to parallel in modern times. Confrontation and violence are the order of the day, not only between nations but also within societies of individual nations. Civilized and honourable behaviour are giving way to anarchy and selfishness everywhere. Kindness and consideration by man for his fellow man, whether their views on various important matters are widely divergent or not, have all but disappeared. The spirit of conciliation and noble gestures in modifying rigid stances in the larger interests of peace and goodwill are invaluable ingredients missing from the mix of present-day society.

Unity is certainly the most valuable commodity that the world needs, but the question is, how do we achieve it? We can't place an order for it with some manufacturer, for we would not know what specifications to give with our order. Even if we did, unity is not something that can be fabricated like a material good. Economics is called the queen of the social sciences, yet even she, with all her knowledge of supply and demand, cannot bring about the equilibrium that the world needs today. What, then, is the answer? Obviously, there can be no simple remedy, but if we turn to the words of Sant Kirpal Singh, he points the way briefly and to the point in the following words. He tells us: 'Unity exists, but we have forgotten.'

When a great saint like Sant Kirpal Singh expresses in a few short words what the world's greatest philosophers could not put better in a thousand page volume, we may be sure that each word contains a mine of important information, which is well worth our while to dig up and smelter for the precious ore that lies therein. 'Unity exists, but we have forgotten.' What does the Master mean by 'unity'? Is it unity of social bodies and institutions? Is it economic unity of nations for the betterment of all, or is it unity of religions? However, when the Master speaks of unity, we know from the forthcoming conference, that he means the 'Unity of Man'.

Unity of Man cannot be achieved by any organization, be it religious, social or political, for all too often, we observe that such organizations are a cause of disunity. When the Master tells us that we have forgotten what unity is, he is talking at the level of the individual soul in man, not the aims and objects of the various organizations. Therefore, it follows that we have forgotten the unity within our own selves, and if we can but recapture it, unity of mankind will follow as a matter of course. In trying to unite mankind in the outer way, we have put the cart before the horse. We must first achieve unity within our own selves. This, then, is the spiritual problem that the Master lays before us, and indeed, is what he has dedicated his whole life to in helping us solve. To further show that it is unity of man as a whole individual to which the Master is directing our attention, let us consider the following factors.

Man is a tripartite being. He has a body, mind, and soul. If all three were acting in unison, there would be no problem, but unfortunately, most of us are only functioning at body consciousness. We know something of the mind, but precious little of our soul. When a single being such as man is composed of three major parts, and these parts are not functioning in unison, it is not surprising that numerous such beings cannot function in unison. If one part of a large and complex piece of machinery breaks down, the whole machinery is brought to a stop. So it follows that we cannot possibly achieve unity among mankind until we start with ourselves. By beginning the work of the integration of our own tripartite self, we are, at the same time, helping greatly to achieve the integration, or unity, of mankind as a whole.

You may agree it is a matter of common sense, that before we can put something into practice, we must either learn the basic theory, or if we have forgotten, then review what we once learnt. Man will only begin to be on the road towards unity when individually, he begins to restore harmony in his own being.

Another question is, why do we forget? Well, if I were to be facetious, I should say it is because we never try to remember. But remembering something requires that we not merely try to recall it; it requires the practice of the virtues which, we are taught, lead to unity. If we do not continually practise what we are taught, we are bound to forget it. If we strive to unite the separate parts of our own being at the level of the soul, as advised by the Master, what begins as remembrance will lead to enlightenment. So when the Master tells us that: 'Unity exists, but we have forgotten', he is also saying that we cannot have unity of man until we have individual enlightenment to a greater or lesser degree.

One of the Upanishadic texts says: 'Lead us from the unreal to the real, and from darkness to light.' If we are living an unreal existence, we are living in darkness, and if we are living in darkness, then we have forgotten our basic unity. Wherever we turn, the same problem confronts us. The Master also tells us that it is a 'man problem', to be solved by man, given of course, the right guidance. But as the world religions demonstrate, there has been no lack of such guidance in the past. Then why haven't we solved the problem?

The coming conference represents a wonderful opportunity given to all delegates to make a major and solid contribution to world peace and harmony. The theme of the conference should not be allowed to degenerate into the mere uttering of cliches. Unity of Man is the noblest concept that can be placed before any organization. The title of the conference consists of three words. Similarly, man consists of three parts. If we all make a major effort to achieve harmony of these separate parts, what will be left? 'UNITY!' If all delegates can keep in mind the noble purpose of the conference, each one will ponder anew on the mysterious workings of his own being. There will be no need to make loud and impassioned speeches as to why 'Unity of Man' should be our goal, for indeed, unity will already exist, and as the Master put it, whatever exists is made manifest, and shines out from the hearts and minds of men.

A SPIRITUAL CONUNDRUM

In the spiritual classic, The Cloud of Unknowing (The Cloud), written by an anonymous English monk in the late fourteenth century, in Chapter II, the author advises a monk who has chosen the religious vocation as a contemplative solitary (one who has undertaken to spend much of his time in prayer):

> "Press on then with speed, I pray you. Look ahead now and never mind what is behind; ...... Now you have to stand in desire, all your lifelong, if you are to make progress in the way of perfection. This desire must be always be at work in your will, by the power of almighty God and by your own consent. ...... Your part is to keep the windows and the door against the inroads of flies and enemies. And if you are willing to do this, **all that is required of you is to woo him humbly in prayer**, and at once he will help you. ...... He is always most willing, and is only waiting for you. So, what are you going to do? How will you move Him?"

In my opinion, there are few indeed who, in the words of the author of The Cloud: "....woo him humbly in prayer.....". And this is so whether they are members of a Religious Order or not, what to speak of the ordinary priest or the non-contemplative religious lay person. This, then, begs the question in respect of the millions upon millions of ordinary souls who struggle through life, but still believe in a loving God; also, the millions upon millions of souls who go through life without any faith whatsoever in a loving, beneficent Creator who desires their salvation. Neither of these two classes understand, let alone practise, prayer in any form. Indeed, they do not comprehend the necessity of prayer at all. Are they, then, all damned? And have the billions upon billions of souls who have long left this physical life been consigned to a state of hell as a result of their indifference in leading a life that focused almost entirely on their physical existence, and which ignored their spiritual self? If this were so, then Satan's kingdom would be infinitely more populated than the Kingdom of Heaven. So, what is the answer to this spiritual conundrum, if there is any answer at all?

It is Scripture that provides the answer, specifically, in the book of the prophet Isaias, verses 8 and 9 of chapter 55, wherein we are told:

> "For my thoughts are not your thoughts: nor your ways my ways, saith the Lord. For as the heavens are exalted above the earth, so are my ways exalted above your ways, and my thoughts above your thoughts."

But this does not mean that we can do as we like and get away with it. For in verses 6 and 7 of the same chapter 55, we are told:

> "Seek ye the Lord while he may be found: call upon him while he is near. Let the wicked forsake his way and the unjust man his thoughts, and let him return to the Lord; and he will have mercy on him: and to our God; for he is bountiful to forgive."

It is in this physical life that the Lord may be found, and when He is more near to us than we are to ourselves. It is in this life that we can merit, not after death. This is clearly set out in verses 17/21 of chapter 3 of the book of the prophet Ezechiel:

"Son of man, I have made thee a watchman to the house of Israel: and thou shalt hear the word out of my mouth and shalt tell it them from me. If, when I say to the wicked, Thou shalt surely die: thou declare it not to him nor speak to him that he may be converted from his wicked way and live, the same wicked man shall die in his iniquity but I will require his blood at thy hand. But if thou give warning to the wicked, and he be not converted from his wickedness and from his evil way: he indeed shall die in his iniquity but thou hast delivered thy soul. Moreover, if the just man shall turn away from his justice and shall commit iniquity: I will lay a stumbling-block before him. He shall die, because thou hast not given him warning. He shall die in his sin and his justices which he hath done, shall not be remembered. But I will require his blood at thy hand. But if thou warn the just man, that the just may not sin, and he doth not sin: living he shall live because thou hast warned him, and thou hast delivered thy soul."

So, if God may be found in this physical life, but few have the time, or the inclination, to spend some time in prayer, then if we strive to live the life of the 'just man' who does not sin, is that good enough? This is not to say that the 'just man' goes through life without sinning, but if he repents and changes his ways, then it is my understanding from the book of the prophet Ezechiel that God will forgive him.

Life is difficult; there are so many legitimate demands in living it in this world, that even good people who believe in God and the afterlife do not have the time or the inclination to pray. The soul, inhabiting the physical body, is separated from God. Therefore, suffering, whether physical, mental or spiritual, is unavoidable. Such suffering, in all three of these aspects, is a form of prayer to be offered up to God. **And it is also my opinion that the very effort we put in to live a good, pure life in this world is itself a form of prayer,** but though I think that this is true, even a good life well lived is not a substitute for prayer itself, **for prayer is our heart speaking to the heart of God.** This is why I encourage all to spend at least half an hour each day in speaking to God, heart to heart. As I have written elsewhere, we usually begin our prayer life with the type of prayer which gives us the most satisfaction, and which occupies the mind, such as oral prayer, or discursive meditation. But the saints tell us that to truly progress, we must go beyond this type of prayer to what is termed the prayer of recollection, or silent prayer, or contemplative prayer. In this way, we speak to God as our best friend. When we do this, we are then led onward by God Himself.

To conclude, if we strive to do this, then we not only greatly benefit our own souls, but also the souls of our nearest and dearest, and even the souls of those whom we do not know; this understanding is enshrined in Isaias 55:8/9 quoted above.

ON GENESIS - CHAPTERS 1 TO 5

Reading Genesis 1:27, 2:20/22, 3:6/12 and 5:2 on the creation of male and female, it is to be noted that God called their name "Adam" in the day when they were created (Genesis 5:2). Therefore, it is clear that the female sex partakes of the gifts and qualities of the male sex in addition to the gifts and qualities of their own sex. From this, we may draw the conclusion that in certain respects, the female sex is superior to the male sex. Also, the female sex often suffers more and carries a greater burden than the male sex. For example, when the woman conceives a child, both husband and wife have their bit of pleasure, but it is the woman who carries the child in her womb and eventually gives birth, often in great pain, after nine months; and it is the woman who carries the greater burden in raising the child, especially in the tasks of cleaning and feeding the child.

The allegory of Adam and Eve also describes the superiority of the woman in Genesis 3:6/12, where it is described how Eve, at the behest of the serpent (Satan), took of the fruit of the tree (of good and evil) in the midst of Paradise, and after eating of it, gave it to her husband, Adam, who took it from her without a murmur (Genesis 3:6). Adam did not say: 'Eve, the Lord said we were not to eat of the fruit of the tree', but took it from her hand like a little lamb and ate of it himself. However, in spite of her innate superiority, the woman has the fault that she can be a bit bossy, and this is why the Lord made her subject to the man (Genesis 3:16).

The opening chapters of the book of Genesis contain marvellous allegories most difficult to comprehend, including the story of Creation and those of Adam and Eve, which from our point of view are perhaps, the most profound, in that the creation of Adam and Eve, representing male and female, also tells us that the male and female principles exist in God Himself. This is my understanding of Genesis 1:27, in which we are told:

'And God created man to his own image; to the image of God he created him. Male and female he created them.' So our destiny is a most glorious one, one that we should always keep in mind as we travel this road we call life. For, in the words of Genesis 3:19: 'In the sweat of thy face shalt thou eat bread till thou return to the earth, out of which thou wast taken: for dust thou art, and unto dust thou shalt return.'

A MYTH IS A FACT FORGOTTEN

A myth is a fact forgotten,
A happening hidden in the mists
of time,
From the womb of God, were we
all begotten,
The soul yearns to return but is
Covered with grime.

From the egg of eternity was born
The child of Infinity;
How can this mystery be grasped by
The mind of man?
Steeped in sin for all his span.

O Infinity of Space;
O Eternity of Time;
Why do we forsake Thee for
The sake of worldly slime?

Philosophers argue, theologians
dispute,
Sensuality entices, the world is its
root.
Scholars debate, they fill books with
effusions,
Then to make confusion confounded
they pass resolutions
On the attributes of God to prove
their delusions.

Those who scoff, or do not care,
Will find themselves caught in
Satan's lair,
Wherein dwell only hopelessness, and
despair.

Those who say, 'I have not the energy
nor the time,
To read this long, meandering rhyme';
Do not accuse me of wasting your time.
The choice is yours, the will
is key,
It can keep you bound, or set
you free.

Now, hearken to a soul, that made its
plaint to the Celestial Three,
This soul came one day to a place
of calm,
Full green, with grassy sward;
But betwixt the soul and it a mighty river
roared,
White-foamed, and in a chasm deep and broad.

Why hast thou brought me here O Lord?
The soul it cried;
Will my search for Thee never cease?
I've read books on books; for years
I've tried
To make sense of life, and find
some peace.

Far off, it seemed, came a bell-like voice,
in answer to my call.
Why blamest thou Me for thy present
thrall?
Which this chasm and this flood do
symbolise;
Who committed those deeds which do us
separate?
Who thinks those thoughts that are in
constant spate?

Souls seek Me, but do not find,
They look without, and not within;
The blind continue to lead the blind,
They disdain not sin, and so do not begin.
Did I not say, My yoke is easy, My
burden light!
But My teachings, man continues to slight.

Man's object in life is to seek pleasure,
He indulges in vice without thought and
no measure;
God, he has consigned to the dust of
the past,
As a sop for the old, the simple, and a
belief that can't last.

In the centuries past, I made known My Will,
But man, glorying in his intellect, despises
it still.
He has deified his mind, and the power of his reason,
A base act of idolatry, the worst type of
treason.

Know that the light of the mind
Is but a reflection
Of the rays of My Thought
Meant for man's sanctification.
Purity is needed to enter My Spheres;
The Victor is he, who still perseveres.

But man's will, now a slave to this appetite, that passion,
Has lost its resilience, its power of rejection
Of the things which keep his soul in subjection
To the body and mind, which most need correction.

Now this gift of My Light
In man's soul has been darkened,
My prophets and saints, to them you've not hearkened.
But the worst crime of all, which brooks no exemption,
Is your denial of Me, and My Act of Redemption.

Man still does not comprehend, the depths of My Sacrifice,
Of what I surrendered at the time of My Passion.
That Cup I asked My Father to take from My lips,
Was not My cruel death, which man's hands did but fashion.

My last words on the Cross completed
the story
Of that Act, which for man fallen opened
the Way for his glory,
Whereby all who ask may be forgiven
So that of vile sin their souls may
be shriven.

For this cause I took form in the Man-body,
A folly of Love, since for one brief moment
of time
I surrendered My Godhood to My Father
in Heaven.
This was the height of My Sacrifice,
a sure Divine Leaven,
Which combined with My Blood, is the
sign of Christ Risen.

Thus was created the Gateway of Mercy,
Which is open to all,
And thus did I atone for the effects of the Fall.
I am no myth, but I have been forgotten.
The remedy is for man to turn back to God
and repent of self-love,
with which like a drunkard he's fully
besotten.

A brief space of time still exists in which
Man must now pause,
and entreat My Forgiveness and obey My
just laws;
I ask that you reflect on My words for
The Day is now yours.

A VERSE ON THE TRINITY

O blessed, blessed Trinity
Who can measure Thy Infinity
Who can comprehend Thy Leniency
Towards our poor humanity
Destined to adore Thy Wondrous Majesty

AUTHOR PROFILE

The author and his wife, who were married in 1963 in Toronto, Canada, went to Old Delhi, India, in 1964 to study spirituality under the guidance of a guru, known as Master Kirpal Singh. They lived in his Ashram for six years, and during that entire time, the author was employed at the Canadian High Commission in New Delhi, on their local staff. Under the guidance of Master Kirpal, they practised the outer or active spiritual disciplines, and the inner spiritual discipline, which focused on the practice of contemplative prayer. They both returned to Canada in 1970, in which year they became Canadian Citizens.

In 1972, because he knew that he was soon to depart from this world, Master Kirpal asked the author's wife to return to India to look after the many Western disciples who would flock there once they heard about this. The author was unable to accompany his wife because he was in the fourth year of his professional accountancy programme. The author also specialised in Canadian income taxation, and was subsequently employed with Revenue Canada as a senior auditor in their Advance Rulings Directorate, which issued binding tax rulings to businesses both large and small.

It was while the author's wife was in India, that he experienced a beautiful vision while in a deep sleep state, in which the understanding was given to him that the Lord desired that both he and his wife enter the Catholic Faith. Although he had this vision in late 1972 or early 1973, it was not until 1992 that they became Catholics. The author's understanding of this is that one enters the state that he refers to as the "Timeless" when one has such an experience. He also adds that visions are not at all necessary to progress spiritually.

Master Kirpal left this world one week before the author arrived in India to join his wife, and they both returned to Canada shortly afterward. For many years, including the time when he and his wife were with Master Kirpal, the author was devoted to the writings of St. John of the Cross, St. Teresa of Avila, St. Francis de Sales, Johann Tauler, and many others who wrote from actual (religious) experience, including Thomas A Kempis, who wrote the Imitation of Christ.